Deindustrialization in Chile

Deindustrialization in Chile

Jaime Gatica Barros

Routledge
Taylor & Francis Group
LONDON AND NEW YORK

First published © 1989 by Westview Press, Inc.

Published 2018 by Routledge
52 Vanderbilt Avenue, New York, NY 10017
2 Park Square, Milton Park, Abingdon, Oxon OX14 4RN

Routledge is an imprint of the Taylor & Francis Group, an informa business

Library of Congress Cataloging-in-Publication Data
Gatica Barros, Jaime.
Deindustrialization in Chile.
(Westview special studies on Latin America and the Caribbean)
Bibliography: p.
Includes index.
1. Chile—Manufactures. 2. Chile—Industries.
3. Industry and state—Chile. 4. Monetary policy—Chile. 5. Chile—Economic policy. I. Title.
II. Series.
HD9734.C52G37 1989 338.983 86-32513

ISBN 13: 978-0-367-01408-7 (hbk)

ISBN 13: 978-0-367-16395-2 (pbk)

To Alejandra, Camila,
and Damian

Contents

Illustrations

Tables

Diagrams

Acknowledgments

Many people contributed to the accomplishment of this book. My major debts are to Victor Tokman, Kenneth Jameson, and Alejandro Foxley. They encouraged me during the crucial early stages and provided helpful suggestions and extensive comments on earlier versions. I would also like to thank my colleagues at PREALC (International Labor Office–Regional Employment Program for Latin America and the Caribbean) for their comments at seminars where the first drafts of some chapters were presented. Among those I especially wish to thank are my friends Alvaro Garcia, Molly Pollack, and Andras Uthoff, with whom I wrote various working papers for PREALC regarding the performance of the Chilean manufacturing sector. My thanks also to Emilio Klein, Carlos Ominami, John Wells, and Mario Castillo for our meaningful conversations regarding the role played by industry during the Chilean monetarist experiment.

I am deeply grateful to my professors at Notre Dame who read early versions of chapters and gave constructive criticism, especially James Rakowski, David Ruccio, and Roger Skurski, and to the Holy Cross Congregation at Notre Dame, particularly to Fathers Ernest Bartell, Richard Warnner, and Gerald Whelan for their support and trust during my graduate studies and research.

A very important word of appreciation goes to my wife, Alejandra, for providing me with the energy and stamina needed to finish writing the book and for reading the manuscript and providing valuable suggestions.

A special word of gratitude goes to Carol de Andrade Pinto for her patience and accuracy in editing the book and to Maria de Fátima Marra for her efficient typing and coding of several versions of the manuscript. My thanks also go to Langston James Goree VI for his excellent computer work in preparing the tables in camera-ready form.

A final word of appreciation goes to my fellow Chilean dissident economists for the research they have done. As acknowledged throughout the text, without their serious and rigorous criticism of the economic policies in Chile of the past 15 years—and their efforts to develop an alternative economic program to the orthodoxy born in 1973—this book would not have been possible.

Jaime Gatica

Introduction

This book analyzes the performance of the manufacturing sector in Chile from 1974 to 1982, looking specifically at the effect of the "neoconservative" or "monetarist experiment" implemented in Chile during that period on the behavior of the Chilean industrial sector.[1] It also examines the period of recovery that began in 1984 when the experiment had ended.

Several authors have pointed to the anti-industrial biases of the "Chilean model."[2] They argue that policies that suddenly encouraged international trade and stringent price stabilization policies, within the context of free markets and a great reduction in the role of government, not only reduced the relative importance of the industrial sector but also significantly restructured it. Some even argue that the effects of the "monetarist experiment" on the industrial sector were more far-reaching. Essentially, the phenomenon of "deindustrialization" occurred, which resulted in the deterioration of an important part of the industrial base of the country.[3]

My aim is to assess the phenomenon of deindustrialization in two ways: first, to measure the relative importance of deindustrialization in terms of the performance of the industrial sector; and second, to analyze the causes of deindustrialization by looking at the resource reallocation pattern induced by monetarist policies and their effects on the industrial structure. The purpose here is to assess empirically the impact of "neoconservative" structural policies on the composition of manufacturing among industrial sectors. I assess the empirical relevance of deindustrialization, identify its causes, and evaluate its economic consequences.

The post-1973 Chilean "stabilization experience" induced a process of deindustrialization that had the following characteristics: an absolute reduction in manufacturing jobs, contraction of the sector's ability to generate foreign exchange, relatively low investment rates, and a reduction in productive capacity. In other words, the transformations that occurred in the Chilean economy from 1974 to 1982 reduced the capacity of the sector to generate employment, thus contributing to an increase in overall unemployment. Deindustrialization not only reduced manufacturing productive capacity, but also reduced the relative contribution of manufacturing to Chilean net exports, which increased pressure on the balance of payments.

Another goal of this book is to examine the performance of the industrial sector during the post-1973 Chilean stabilization experience in two important ways. First, by evaluating the effects that deindustrialization has on short-term economic recovery; and second, by providing a framework for addressing the issues of long term industrialization. The particular characteristics of the "orthodox" Chilean stabilization experience make the Chilean case the purest example among those developing countries that have attempted to apply similar policies. In Chile, policy measures based on a "monetarist" theoretical concept of the functioning and adjustment of the economy were applied rigorously.

Additionally, because Chile has been ruled by a military dictatorship since September 1973, government economists have had an exceptional degree of autonomy in designing, putting into practice, and adjusting economic policies over an extended period of time. Thus, a clearer assessment of the model is possible.

From an analytical point of view, this book breaks down the deindustrialization process into component parts and examines the empirical evidence, using different methodologies to assess the degree and magnitude of deindustrialization. Official government statistics, interviews with government officials and entrepreneurs, and quantitative methods were used to estimate and measure specific issues relevant to the deindustrialization phenomenon.

The book is divided into six chapters. The focus of Chapter 1 is on the theoretical issues underlying the study of deindustrialization. The importance of manufacturing for economic development is emphasized, as are the conditions under which deindustrialization can be understood as a structural "mal-adjustment" of the economy. I then briefly present the theoretical foundations upon which the "neoconservative model" was built and its strategic elements. The focus is on the order and intensity with which the post-1973 stabilization and liberalization policies were applied and on how they affected the performance of the manufacturing sector.

In Chapter 2 I present the relevant indicators available to measure Chilean deindustrialization. The first section of the chapter begins by looking at the relative shares of manufacturing output and employment from 1974 until 1982. I assess the results by examining the performance of industrial output and employment in Chile during the 1960s and in other developing and Latin American countries. An attempt is made to quantify the costs of the "monetarist model" in terms of manufacturing output and employment. I estimate the loss of industrial output by comparing actual with potential production. An analysis of the reduction in industrial productive capacity follows. Then, after briefly discussing problems associated with different methods used in the literature to estimate capacity output, a formal presentation is made of an adapted version of the "trends through peaks" or "Wharton method." The flaws and advantages of this method are also discussed here. Estimates are given for manufacturing groups disaggregated at a three-digit level of the International Standard Industrial Classification revision 2 (ISIC rev. 2). Additional empirical information is given concerning the decline of the nation's manufacturing base. Two types of indicators, the evolution of the number of bankruptcies and the number of establishments, are used. I then analyze the changes in the composition of manufacturing employment disaggregated by manufacturing groups (three-digit, ISIC rev. 2). Finally, the main conclusions are presented, including an analysis of the impact on the whole manufacturing sector and identification of those manufacturing groups that were most affected by the deindustrialization process.

The objective of the second section of Chapter 2 is to analyze whether the changes occurring in the manufacturing sector should be perceived as a movement towards greater efficiency—in other words, to empirically assess to what extent the neoconservative policies were successful in taking resources away from inefficient activities and putting them into more productive ones. Three criteria are used to analyze this issue. First, I look at the changes in the structure of employment among economic activities; second, I analyze the contribution of manufacturing to the external commercial balance; and third, I look at changes in productivity and investment.

There were basically two structural policies inherent in the "neoconservative model": first, the sudden removal of barriers to international trade; and second, the liberalization of domestic capital markets and openness to external financial markets. In Chapter 3 I study the impact these two major structural policies had on the industrial sector, analyzing whether the changes they induced did actually produce the resource reallocation pattern assumed by the model. The chapter begins with a general description of the policies implemented to open the economy to international trade. I then present the methodology used to measure the sources of structural change among manufacturing groups. The objective is to quantify the relative impact of the opening up process on industrial groups. The method is an extended version of the Chenery (1980) model which allows one to identify the relative contribution to gross output of three major effects: the net changes occurring in domestic demand, in exports, and in imports. With this analysis it is possible to identify whether the changes were due to internal or external factors and, among the latter, to differentiate between the net contributions of exports and imports.

In the second section of this chapter, I analyze the impact of the financial liberalization process on manufacturing firms. The objective is to determine if and how the financial reforms altered the behavior of firms and affected their functions. The main characteristics of the financial reforms are described, along with their effects on the functioning of the capital market. I then focus on the financial behavior of bankrupt firms at a more microeconomic level, comparing their financial indicators with those of firms that survived. Specifically, I look at the balance sheets of a sample of firms that went bankrupt and calculate liquidity, profitability and debt indicators, comparing them with those of the firms that were able to remain operational.

Chapter 4 supports thc analysis of the previous chapters with qualitative information based on case studies. I first analyze the bankruptcy procedure and its implications for the study of deindustrialization. Information was directly gathered from the government agency in charge of supervising bankruptcies and from interviews with government officials and managers of firms that went bankrupt. I then take a closer look at the reactions experienced and adjustments made by bankrupt manufacturing firms. The purpose is to identify the problems these firms faced and the adjustments made in their production processes and financial management.

Chapter 5 analyzes whether the performance of the industrial sector during the recovery of 1984–1986 reinforces the deindustrialization hypothesis. I also briefly discuss changes in the economic policies which occurred after the 1982 crisis, and how these policies affected industry's recovery.

The conclusions and implications of the study are presented in Chapter 6. Two sets of related issues are analyzed here. First, the type of constraints that deindustrialization imposes on short-term economic recovery; and second, the main elements involved in a "reindustrialization" strategy.

Notes

1. The economic model followed in Chile from September of 1973 until June of 1982 has been called many names in the literature, including the "Chicago Experiment," "Monetarist Model," "Global Monetarist Model," and "Orthodox Model." Even though each name reflects, to a certain extent, a

particular way of interpreting and understanding the economic events of those years, I will use them interchangeably.

2. See, among others, Vergara (1980), Ffrench-Davis (1979), CIEPLAN (1984), Duran (1980), Pinto (1981), and PREALC (1984).

3. This argument was developed especially after the recession of 1982. See PREALC (1984), Tokman (1984), AES (1984), and Muñoz (1982).

1

Theoretical Issues in the Study of Deindustrialization

The concept of deindustrialization as applied to a country like Chile raises a whole set of complex questions. First, how important is the manufacturing sector to economic development? What is so special about industry that deindustrialization should cause such concern? This research was born out of a special concern about the performance of manufacturing during the neoconservative experiment. That concern seems justified by the literature on the importance of industry in economic development, some of which is reviewed in the next section.

One theoretical issue relates to the meaning of deindustrialization and the conditions under which it can be understood as a structural "mal-adjustment" of the economy. This point is especially relevant for a small developing country like Chile, which was put through a rapid-fire combination of policy measures that drastically changed the structure and functioning of its economy. This is the very basic and fundamental issue which will be present throughout the book. What were the characteristics of the so-called Chilean neoconservative experiment and what type of resource reallocation process was induced by this experiment? Our main concern is whether or not the neoconservative policies actually led to greater efficiency in the use and allocation of productive resources. In other words, should the deindustrialization phenomenon be considered a normal adjustment process in which resources are moved from inefficient activities to more productive ones?

Thus, a major aim of this book is to articulate and examine empirically a line of reasoning which has been put forth to explain how and why deindustrialization occurs. The argument is that the combination of restrictive monetary and fiscal policies, price and interest rate deregulation, and policies that suddenly allow and encourage international trade and exchange with foreign financial markets, all set against the background of an authoritarian military government, produced an economic environment strongly inhibitive to the manufacturing sector. Closely related are the issues associated with the different interpretations of the concept of deindustrialization and the empirical methodologies used to measure that concept.

In the next section I approach these problems looking at two main issues: the meaning of deindustrialization and the relationship between the changes in productive efficiency and deindustrialization. Next, I analyze how these issues relate to the Chilean case. Specifically I look at the economic policies that were applied in Chile from 1974 to 1982 and the process of resource reallocation that was generated by these policies. The objective is to contrast the intended with the unintended results of the policy measures and to analyze their consequent impact on the manufacturing sector.

The Importance of Manufacturing in Economic Development

Why should one be particularly concerned about the performance of the industrial sector? In the case of Chile, there are practical and theoretical reasons. Regarding the latter, there is extensive literature justifying the importance of industry to economic development.[1] Here, I will briefly present the major arguments for developing the industrial sector to promote dynamic economic growth.

The importance of manufacturing to economic development can be seen by examining the historical development of capitalism, especially in the developed countries. Industry played a central role in determining their growth in output and employment. Cripps and Tarling (1973) studied the growth process in advanced industrialized countries from 1950 to 1970, and their results confirmed Kaldor's hypothesis that there is a close relationship between the growth rate of a country's GDP and the growth of its manufacturing sector. Therefore, a downturn in manufacturing is a matter of concern.

Moreover, manufacturing's contribution to economic development increases when one considers the multiplier effects that industry has on other economic sectors. Manufacturing backward linkages in the production of inputs and forward linkages in the marketing process. Thus, its expansion has a considerable effect on other phases of production and sales.

Furthermore, in the manufacturing sector it is possible to make relatively better use of economies of scale and technical progress, both of which increase productivity and provide higher incomes and better work opportunities. Also, the chain of relationships between manufacturing and other economic sectors facilitates the transmission of these positive effects to the rest of the economy.

Very much related to the previous point, it is argued that the industrial sector plays a key role in increasing productivity and productive employment. Given the relatively larger income elasticity of demand for manufactured goods, a faster growth rate is expected in industry than in other sectors. Because of the existence of economies of scale, manufacturing growth is usually associated with employment expansion at greater productivity levels. In agriculture and services, however, productivity growth is generally associated with reductions in employment. Consequently, as the overall growth rate of productivity in developed countries accelerates, industrial employment expands while non-manufacturing employment falls.

The expansion of manufacturing indirectly, but importantly, affects the labor market. On one hand, the interrelationship of production and technology induces the development of activities thoughout the economy. Direct employment is generated by the production of final manufactured goods and indirect employment by the production of inputs and in the process of marketing those goods. Garcia (1982) estimated that in 1970 the employment multiplier in the manufacturing sector of six Latin American countries (representing 70 percent of total Latin American employment in manufacturing) was above two. This means that for every job created in industry, another is created elsewhere in the economy. Additionally, this same author estimated that direct and indirect manufacturing employment accounts for 35 to 40 percent of total employment in these six countries.

Another point is the fact that capital productivity is greater in manufacturing than in other sectors. Manufacturing generates a relatively greater level of profits, allowing for increased investments and a greater rate of growth. In other words, the potential for raising output and employment is greater in the manufacturing sector than in other economic activities.

Additionally, the industrialization process generates qualitative changes in the type of employment demanded. Technological change as well as the greater complexity of industrial jobs creates on-the-job learning, resulting in a more highly skilled manufacturing labor force. The structure of manufacturing production processes requires greater specialization from employers and opens more opportunities for upward mobility.

The greater labor productivity generated in the sector also allows higher wages. This is clearly observed when comparing industrial with agricultural jobs. In the latter, the required qualifications of the labor force are low and the stratification by type of job is limited. In manufacturing, job diversity is greater, allowing for specialization and upward mobility.

Regarding the importance of short-run macroeconomic stability to developing countries, it is important to point out manufacturing's potential capacity for alleviating the recurrent external imbalance, and thus reducing the economy's vulnerability to external shocks.

In addition to these theoretical bases there are two important practical reasons that justify the study of deindustrialization in Chile. First, for whatever reasons and regardless of the characteristics of its industrial development process in the 1950s and 1960s, the fact is that by 1973 the Chilean economy had developed a substantial industrial production base. Considering the subsequent enormous changes that occurred in Chile's economy from 1974 to 1982, this fact in itself justifies an analysis of the industrial sector during the neoconservative experiment.

Second, as analyzed in the next chapters, one of the goals of the neoconservative policies was to generate efficient productive activities outside the industrial sector. It is interesting to note that, in spite of the intensity with which these policies were implemented, they were incapable of generating these alternative activities. This is a very important fact to consider when assessing the importance of manufacturing in the development process of a country.

Points of Departure for the Study of Deindustrialization

Only during the last decade has the phenomenon of deindustrialization been recognized by the industrialized world. Since then it has been studied in the United Kingdom and more recently in the United States.

It is useful to begin the study of deindustrialization by looking at the varying interpretations this phenomenon has had in this literature.

In a study made in the U.S. by Bluestone and Harrison (1982), deindustrialization is defined as a process associated with a particular form of capital mobility. For these authors deindustrialization is a

> . . . widespread and systematic disinvestment in the nation's basic productive capacity. The essential problem with the U.S. economy can be traced to the way capital—in the forms of financial resources and of real plant and equipment—has been diverted from productive investment in our basic national industries into unproductive speculation, mergers and acquisiton, and foreign investments.

The important point to notice in this definition is the association between deindustrialization and disinvestment; to these authors, deindustrialization is the cause of disinvestment. As we will see below this has important empirical implications. But first, it is important to realize that the meaning of disinvestment is also under dispute. Rakowski (1984) says it can be understood by considering the following:

In what way does the acquisition of existing assets (plants and equipment) reduce available resources for productive investment? For example, if an enterprise decides to use its funds to buy an already existing manufacturing firm, does this mean that less resources will be available for productive investment in terms of the whole economy? What is the relationship between new capital formation and the acquisition of existing assets? If the latter increases, will the former decrease? Using the reasoning behind the basic macroeconomic identity, i.e. saving equals investment, Rakowski (1984) concludes that ". . . in a closed economy taken as a whole, spending of money on already existing assets—gold, gems, established companies, real estate, etc. . . . does not destroy the resources for real investment, as long as saving is not reduced."

In other words, in the aggregate "it is impossible for an economy to lose the investment effects of saving by passing that saving from hand to hand." Rakowski points out, however, that capital could be transferred out of an open economy to other countries, depriving the domestic economy of the productive services of those resources.

The "Cambridge view" emphasizes the meaning of an "efficient manufacturing sector" in an open economy like that of the U.K. Singh (1977) defines an efficient manufacturing sector as one that not only satisfies the demands of consumers at home, but is also able to sell enough of its products abroad to pay for the nation's import requirements.

However, an efficient manufacturing sector must also be able to achieve these objectives at socially acceptable levels of output, employment and exchange rate. Cambridge economists are therefore concerned with the progressive failure to achieve a sufficient surplus of manufactured exports over imports, to keep the economy in external balance and at full employment.

Another way to view changes occurring in the manufacturing sector as a deindustrialization process is the consideration of whether deindustrialization is a normal adjustment process in which resources are moved from inefficient activities to more productive ones. The cases of loss of employment in the industrial sector as a result of deindustrialization are particularly enlightening.

Bluestone and Harrison (1982) contrast what the process of deindustrialization is supposed to do for the economy with its actual consequences.

> . . . an enormous amount of evidence (reveals) that the economic reincarnation process is not working according to the book. Disinvestment is supposed to free labor and capital from relatively unproductive uses in order to put them to work in more productive ones. But very often this is not the case. Virtually all studies of workers who lose their jobs as the result of a plant closing show that a large proportion of the unemployed take years to recover their lost earnings and many never find comparable work at all. These are not merely personal losses, for when a worker is forced out of a high-productivity job into a low-productivity job, all of society suffers. Real productivity goes down when the experienced, skilled autoworker in Flint, Michigan, ends up buffing cars in the local car wash.

Paraphrasing Bluestone and Harrison, the same is true for investment capital. Moving resources out of an obsolete textile mill in the southern town of Tome in Chile into a high productivity fish industry may increase the productivity of those working with the new equipment, and society may benefit from the products of the new industry. This will most definitely not be the case, however, when the resources that are released are either transferred out of the economy, used to import textiles, or used to speculate in financial markets.

Cairncross (1979), in a study on the U.K., refers to this same issue in the following terms:

> If the decline in the share of manufacturing in total employment were balanced by a shift of consumer demand towards services, or if less spending on manufacturing were offset by a higher rate of savings for investment either at home or abroad, there would be no obvious reason for concern. The change in employment would merely reflect this shift in consumer preferences.

Tokman (1984) in his study on Chile and Argentina, says that the decrease in the level of industrial employment and the rise in the number of plant closings could be interpreted as a positive effect pursued by the policy makers. This is because reallocating resources to those sectors that have comparative advantages would necessarily affect an inefficient industrial sector developed under the protection of high tariffs. If the reallocation of resources was successful, the resulting low employment level in the industrial sector should have been compensated for by the creation of high-productivity jobs in non-manufacturing sectors, according to this author.

The relationship between capital mobility and changes in productivity is a crucial issue in the study of deindustrialization. Numerous economic policies claim to be justified in the name of increased efficiency and productivity. Although the policy measures may aim in the right direction, they often fail due to the length and difficulty of the adjustment process required. This is especially common in developing countries like Chile, where markets are imperfect and imbalances sometimes generate short-run results opposite to policy makers' intentions. The consequences are long-lasting and costly adjustments and sometimes the pursued objective is never reached.[2]

The extent to which deindustrialization can be understood as a structural mal-adjustment of the economy has also been analyzed from an open economy perspective. It may well be argued that deindustrialization is a normal phenomenon associated with changes in domestic and world market conditions. This point is especially important in the case of Chile, where the economy was suddenly opened to international trade and financial markets. The question there is whether deindustrialization occurs as a result of integrating the economy into international markets. The empirical test is to see if manufactured imports increased at a much faster rate than exports. This approach was suggested by Singh (1977), where he argues that ". . . in an open economy the question whether deindustrialization can in any sense be regarded as implying structural mal-adjustment cannot be properly considered in terms of the characteristics of the domestic economy alone."

Based on this approach, Tokman (1984) points to the lack of foreign exchange as an important constraint in the Southern Cone countries. This scarcity coupled with a growing external deficit in manufactured goods, not compensated for by increased exports in non-manufacturing sectors, increases the pressure on the overall external balance. Thus, a criterion to analyse whether the performance of the manufacturing sector improved overall economic efficiency is to compare industry's net foreign exchange contribution to international trade to that of non-industrial sectors.

The Chilean Economic Policy Context

For the developing nations, particularly those in Latin America, the issue of industrialization has been central to their economic development process. Led by the policies proposed by the Economic Commission for Latin America (ECLA), most Latin American countries went through a process of import substitution in the 1950s and 1960s. In spite of the problems it raised, import substitution was the main industrial strategy contributing to their industrial development.

However, for some Latin American countries, industrial development broke down during the 1970s. Because of internal political difficulties, along with the problems brought about by import substitution and the changing international situation, the Southern Cone countries—Argentina, Chile and Uruguay—embarked on economic programs that drastically changed their historical development pattern.

A "new orthodoxy" was born. The emphasis was now on free trade according to comparative advantages. Formerly closed economies were opened to international financial markets. The relative size of the government was reduced. Resource allocation was dictated by free market prices and stabilization policies, with inflexible priority given to cutting inflation. The specific form, sequence and intensity of these policies had greatest effect on the industrial sector, particularly in Chile and Argentina. Industrial production was practically stagnant, job loss was concentrated in the industrial sector, and productive investment fell below the already historically poor rates.

In order to understand the causes of the poor performance of the industrial sector, and to identify the type of policies which promoted deindustrialization, this part is devoted to the impact on the industrial sector of the post-1973 Chilean stabilization experience.

The section begins with a general discussion of the strategic objectives of the neoconservative model and the policies implemented to achieve these objectives. I then analyze the specific form, sequence and intensity of these policies. Finally, an attempt is made to identify and classify the major polcies that affected industrial performance during the monetarist experiment.

The development strategy of the neoconservative model had two fundamental objectives: to restore the role of the market and to strengthen the importance of the private sector. Prices set by the free play of supply and demand would be the principal mechanism to determine the allocation of resources, distribution of income, and level of employment.

The counterpart of these objectives was the reduction in importance of the government, which implied reducing its role in production and distribution as well as limiting its other powers. Henceforth, the private sector would be the dynamic force of the economy; the government would limit itself to creating general conditions so that market signals and incentives could operate without distortions or interference.

To achieve these objectives the following policies were applied:

- Because prices should reflect opportunity costs and not distributive objectives, markets were liberalized and price controls eliminated.
- Because the economy should take advantage of economies of scale and comparative advantages, markets were suddenly opened to

international trade, tariffs were rapidly reduced, and (at least at first) a realistic exchange rate policy was adopted.

- Because financial markets were "repressed" in the McKinnon sense, a domestic financial market was developed, interest rates were liberalized, and all quantitative and qualitative controls on credit allocation were eliminated.
- Because the economy should take full advantage of external savings, most restrictions were eliminated on international capital flows and trading on international financial markets.
- Because markets work, all interference with their normal functioning was eliminated, especially organized labor groups. Unions were banned and professional associations were no longer recognized by the government.
- Because the private sector is the dynamic force behind economic growth, the fiscal deficit and the size of the government was quickly reduced.
- Because the most important condition for normal functioning of markets is price stability, the government budget deficit was eliminated, wages were severely repressed, and restrictive monetary and fiscal policies were implemented.

In order to better understand the effects these measures had on the industrial sector, it is useful to classify them into two types: (1) those measures affecting the level of economic activity through changes in aggregate demand via monetary and fiscal policies; and (2) those policies affecting the composition of expenditures through changes in relative prices. As we will explain below, the major effects of the latter policies were the deterioration of international competitiveness, the high real interest rates, and shifts in the "system of incentives," all of which affected both actual and potential industrial production during this period. In the rest of this section I present a more detailed analysis of how these policies affected the performance of the industrial sector.

Following the approach used by Foxley (1982) and CEPAL (1984), it is possible to identify three phases in the Chilean stabilization experience: Phase I (September 1973–June 1976), Phase II (June 1976–June 1979), and Phase III (June 1979–June 1982).

In the first phase, the main objective was to restore equilibrium in the different markets. Commodity prices were freed in October 1973, the exchange rate was devalued, and interest rates were sharply raised and then deregulated in 1975. However, in order to avoid inflationary pressures and assure the effectiveness of restrictive monetary and fiscal policies, wages were repressed. The combination of restrictive monetary and fiscal policies and the asymmetric price and wage policies led to a sharp decline in employment and industrial production.[3] New policies introduced in the functioning of capital markets generated high real interest rates, further contributing to the fall in industrial production.

At the same time industry's international competitiveness improved due to devaluation of the peso and the drop in real wages. This process was accompanied by gradual tariff reductions, mainly absorbing "redundant protection" during this phase.[4]

The anti-inflationary objective and the belief in the private sector as the dynamic economic force led to sharp reductions in government expenditures and higher taxes. Furthermore, these adjustments in the budget were accompanied by a reduction in the relative size of the government. Public employment decreased sharply, especially in those governmental institutions designed to promote the development of the country's productive capacity.

Public enterprises and private property appropriated by the government during President Salvador Allende's term (1971–1973) were returned to former owners. From an institutional point of view, these were the first signs of a sharp break with the role the government historically played in the Chilean economy.[5]

The second phase (June 1976–June 1979) can be generally characterized by the de-indexation of key prices to break inflationary expectations and thus reduce cost pressures.

In spite of the "shock treatment" implemented in the previous phase, the inflation rate accelerated during the first semester of 1976. With no fiscal deficit and a lower rate of monetary growth, the economic authorities came to the conclusion that inflationary expectations were the driving force behind inflation.

The key variable used to reduce these expectations was the exchange rate. In June 1976 and the first half of 1977 the exchange rate was revalued; inflation decreased from 197.9 percent in 1976 to 84.2 percent in 1977 and to 37.2 percent in 1978. After this success the exchange rate was used as a major stabilization instrument.

This process, together with accelerated tariff reductions and a recovery in real wages, led to a decline in the industrial sector's competitive position as shown by the decline in the real exchange rate. However, at this point, the increase in domestic demand due to increasing real wages had a stronger impact on industrial production, more than offsetting the sector's declining competitive position. This phenomenon explains the recovery of industrial production during this phase.

Another factor which might have helped the competitive position of the industrial sector was the calculation of the inflation rate. It has been argued that miscalculations of the official consumer price index

(CPI) were another reason for reductions in the expansion rate of costs and prices.[6] Since the official CPI was underestimating inflation, and wages and the nominal exchange rate were indexed to it, wages and import prices increased by less than the actual rate of inflation, thus contributing to a lower inflation rate.[7]

Overall, industrial production increased during this phase; large inflows of foreign capital, which lowered domestic real interest rates, further helped the recovery.

Phase Three starts in June 1979 when the exchange rate was fixed in nominal terms. From this point on, the economic authorities expected the economy to follow the predictions of "global monetarism." According to this view, any disequilibrium between income and expenditures is automatically corrected via changes in the interest rate and prices (Whitman, 1975).

In order to contrast the adjustment mechanism predicted by the theory with the real adjustment experienced by the Chilean economy, let us assume that a disequilibrium between income and expenditure is produced by an overall deficit in the balance of payments. The theoretical adjustment mechanism is the following: Reserves will flow out decreasing the money supply and pushing interest rates up, which in turn decrease expenditure. The reduction in aggregated demand produces a decline in imports and drives domestic prices down. Given that the nominal exchange rate is fixed, the deceleration of domestic inflation produces a devaluation of the real exchange rate, further reducing imports and stimulating an increase in exports.[8] The higher domestic interest rates also help reduce the balance of payments deficit by stimulating foreign capital inflows.

The adjustment mechanism actually experienced by the Chilean economy was the following: Fixing the exchange rate reduced inflation. However, the speed at which this process occurred was insufficient to halt the decline in the economy's competitive position. Domestic inflation was greater than external inflation until the second semester of 1981. The result was a rapid appreciation of the real exchange rate and therefore a deterioration in international competitiveness.[9]

However, by the end of 1979 and during 1980, the economy continued to absorb a great amount of foreign resources; reserves accumulated until the end of 1980. During this period aggregate demand was high. Industrial production increased, and in spite of the fact that there was no improvement in industrial employment, the overall unemployment rate slowly declined.

By mid-1981 the situation changed drastically. Lagging competitive ness generated a large trade deficit. Since the nominal exchange rate was still pegged to the dollar, it became apparent that it was overvalued, therefore increasing the expectations of a devaluation. As a result, capital inflows decreased significantly and a deficit in the overall balance of payments was generated. The automatic mechanism began to work. Reserves flowed out, the money supply fell, the interest rate rose and aggregate demand fell. However, the next step of the predicted adjustment, i.e. the fall in domestic prices, was never sufficient to permit a devaluation of the real exchange rate.

Hence, the economy's ability to compete internationally suffered another set-back and the country entered into the second-worst recession of the century. Since the economic authorities insisted on the automatic mechanism as a way out of the recession, and domestic prices did not respond, the revaluation process of the real exchange rate continued and the expectations of devaluation further increased. This in turn produced a further fall in capital inflows and a rise in interest rates.

Both factors contributed to a rapid decline in aggregate demand, employment, and industrial production. Moreover, as a consequence of the overvalued exchange rate, the industrial sector was also affected by a sharp drop in manufacturing exports. The deficit in the balance of payments reached 90 percent of the export value and the inflow of external credit became absolutely necessary for the functioning of the model. However, these inflows were abruptly stopped when the financial bubble burst at the end of 1981. It was impossible for firms to continue paying annual average real interest rates of 25 to 30 percent, while during the six previous years (1975–1981) output had grown at an average real annual rate of only seven percent.[10]

The general deterioration of productive activities, the increasing revaluation of the peso, and the high interest rates led to an increase in domestic unpaid loans. By the end of 1981, banks' bad loans represented 25 percent of their capital and reserves, threatening the bankruptcy of the entire financial system. That threat was only avoided through government intervention at eight financial institutions in November 1981. However, this was the signal external banks needed to drastically reduce their own loans.

In June 1982 the exchange rate was devalued. However, the events that followed confirmed the fact that the devaluation was "too little, too late." The loss of confidence produced a run on the peso which was followed by a sharp reduction in reserves, and hence of the money supply, fueling the recession. In August 1982 the government shifted to a floating exchange rate but in September fixed it again, this time to a basket of currencies using a "crawling-peg" system.[11]

To summarize, the performance of the industrial sector has been determined by four major factors since 1973: First were the changes in the level of industrial activity produced by those policies which affected aggregate demand. Especially important in this respect was the tight monetary policy followed during the whole period, although most strongly enforced during the first phase of the stabilization program. The rapid reduction in government expenditures also contributed to the decline in aggregate demand.

The other factors are related to those policies which changed relative prices and thus the composition of expenditures. The first of these is the loss in international competitiveness which was induced by the rapid reduction of tariffs and the overvalued exchange rate. Without protectionist tariffs a process of de-substitution of imports occurred that was not at all compensated for by manufacturing exports.[12] The overvalued exchange rate was due to the fixed exchange rate policy implemented during the third phase of the program.

High real interest rates were the third factor that affected industrial production. Important changes in the functioning of capital markets determined, "inter-alia," positive and high real interest rates. Industrial entrepreneurs, accustomed to working with a high percentage of borrowed capital and negative real interest rates, were particularly affected by these changes. The high real interest rates coupled with heavy indebtedeness produced a financial burden of such magnitude that by 1982 many firms went bankrupt. This phenomenon became particularly crucial at the beginning of 1983, when the government had to intervene in the major financial institutions and commercial banks to prevent the breakdown of the entire financial sector.

The last factor explaining the relative decline of the industrial sector is the change in the "system of incentives" in the economy. Most possibilities for making high profits were of a short-term nature. The loss in competitiveness shifted resources to the non-tradable sectors and allowed incomes associated with imports to increase. More important, the extraordinarily high interest rates shifted resources from the productive sector to financial speculation, as the rates of return offered by the latter were impossible to attain in the former. In other words, the "system of incentives" was biased against productive investment and strongly encouraged financial speculation. As we will see in the next chapter, this phenomenon partly explains the low investment rates observed during the entire period.

Overall, the loss in competitiveness, deficits in the balance of payments, and extremely high interest rates, together produced by 1982 a sharp fall in employment and industrial production, with a record number of bankruptcies and plant closings.

Notes

1. See Kaldor (1966, 1967); Cripps and Tarling (1973); Boyer and Petit (1981); Singh (1982). See Pinto (1983) for a recent analysis of these issues in

Latin America. Some specific country studies are the following: Peru—Jimenez (1982); Mexico—Vazquez (1981); Chile—Muñoz (1982), Weinstein (1984), Garcia (1984), Castillo and Tardito (1984).

2. The most dramatic example of this is the fight against inflation in Chile since 1973. See for example Ramos (1980), the second part of Foxley (1982) and the next section of this chapter.

3. Demand restrictions were so severe, especially in 1975, that the stabilization package became known as the "shock treatment."

4. Redundant protection is used in the following sense: tariffs were so high in September 1973 that when tariff reductions were first implemented, the impact on domestic prices and production was negligible. The Chilean process of import liberalization has been studied by Ffrench-Davis (1980). The impact of trade liberalization on the industrial sector has been studied by Vergara (1980). For an empirical estimate of the impact of trade liberalization on short-term unemployment, see Edwards (1982).

5. See Vergara (1981) for an analysis of changes in the economic functions of the state. A detailed study of government expenditures was made by Marshall (1981). Changes in public employment were studied by Marshall and Romaguera (1981).

6. At this point it is widely recognized that the National Bureau of Statistics (INE) underestimated inflation rates for the years 1973, 1976, 1977 and 1978. An accurate discussion of these errors is made in Ramos (1980) and in Cortazar and Marshall (1980).

7. See Cortazar (1982) and Arellano and Cortazar (1982).

8. The real exchange rate is defined as $e = EP^*/P$ where E = nominal exchange rate (the peso value of one unit of foreign currency). P^* = foreign prices denominated in foreign currency; and P = domestic prices denominated in the domestic currency. See Dornbusch and Fischer (1981), pp. 698–702.

9. See Dornbusch (1980), Chapter 12, for a macroeconomic model where this process is formalized.

10. For an analysis of the role played by the financial sector, see Zahler (1980) and Ffrench-Davis and Arellano (1981).

11. The Chilean recession of 1982 has produced an interesting amount of economic literature. See, among others, Corbo (1982); Arellano and Cortazar (1982); Muñoz (1982) and Flaño (1982).

12. De-substitution of imports occurs as a result of opening the economy to international trade. Imported products replace industrial output previously produced under high levels of protection.

2

The Evolution of the Manufacturing Sector: 1974–1982

The objective of this chapter is to analyze the performance of manufacturing during the neoconservative experiment, emphasizing its effects on productive capacity.

The chapter is divided into two sections. The first section empirically assesses the extent of the decline of the Chilean manufacturing sector by looking at general indicators showing the evolution of employment and industrial output. I then estimate the costs of the monetarist experiment in terms of manufacturing output and employment, comparing actual with potential figures. An estimate of the evolution of productive capacity by industrial groups is made and two indicators are used to measure the degree of capacity deterioration. The focus here is on the evolution of manufacturing bankruptcies and on the decline in the number of establishments. Finally I analyze the changes in the composition of employment by manufacturing groups, before presenting conclusions.

In the second section of this chapter, I make a general evaluation of these changes in light of the objectives pursued by the model. In particular I examine whether the decline of the sector should be interpreted as a movement in the right direction—i.e., that it was the kind of resource reallocation process pursued by the policy makers—or whether the contraction was due to the failure of the model. Three criteria are used to make the assessment: changes in the structure of employment among economic activities, the contribution made by manufacturing to overall external commercial balance, and changes in productivity and investment.

Overall, this chapter shows very poor performance of industrial output and employment during the neoconservative experiment, relative to historical and Latin American standards. Bankruptcies increased sharply, the number of establishments fell significantly, and output capacity severely deteriorated. Moreover, employment losses in the manufacturing sector did not lead to redeployment to other activities, but only to increased overall unemployment.

The industrial sector's capacity to generate foreign exchange was reduced, thus helping increase the imbalance in the country's external sector. Furthermore, the rate of investment decreased compared to historical levels, and productivity did not increase above those figures observed in the past. The analysis of the previous indicators disaggregated by manufacturing groups (three-digit ISIC rev. 2)[1] showed that groups producing regular and durable consumer goods and transport and professional equipment were most affected by deindustrialization.

The Extent of the Decline in Chilean Manufacturing

In this section I look at general indicators attempting to quantify the magnitude and intensity of the decline of the Chilean manufacturing sector during the neoconservative experiment. For each indicator the analysis is made at two levels, for total industry and for manufacturing groups disaggregated at three-digit level ISIC rev. 2, which allows determination of those groups that were most affected by the deindustrialization process. This chapter is mainly descriptive since the sources and causes of the structural changes that occurred in the manufacturing sector are analyzed in detail in Chapter 3.

The Evolution of Employment and Industrial Output

An initial approximation of the evolution in the industrial sector can be made by observing its relative share in national employment and output over time.

The figures presented in Table 2.1 show that the relative share of both industrial employment and output declined from 1970 to 1982. The proportion of industrial production in total output decreased from 24.7 percent in 1970 to 19.3 percent in 1982. (See Table 2.1, column 1.) Between those same years, the share of manufacturing employment in total employment decreased from 21.5 percent to 12.7 percent. (See Table 2.1, column 4.) Because industrial firms are concentrated around the capital, Santiago, the share of industrial employment in total employment in "Gran Santiago" had a larger decrease, from an average of 27.9 percent during 1965–1970 to 18.2 percent in 1982.[2]

The employment index of manufacturing industry calculated by "SOFOFA" also shows a decline.[3] According to this indicator, employment in manufacturing in 1982 was only 70.1 percent of the level

TABLE 2.1 Employment and Industrial Output: 1970-1983

Years	Share of Indust. in Total GDP	Index of Ind. GDP (1970=100)		Share of Indust. in Total Employment		Index of Ind. Employment (1970=100)
	(1)	(2)	(3)	(4)	(5)	(6)
1970	24.7	100.0	100.0	21.5(a)	27.9(b)	100.0
1971	25.7	113.6	-	-	-	102.5
1972	26.6	116.1	-	-	-	110.7
1973	26.0	107.1	-	-	-	113.2
1974	25.1	104.4	108.3	-	26.1	110.4
1975	21.5	77.8	78.1	17.2	24.5	100.0
1976	22.0	82.5	82.0	17.0	24.6	92.6
1977	21.7	89.5	90.2	16.7	24.2	92.1
1978	22.0	97.8	96.9	16.3	23.0	92.0
1979	21.9	105.5	104.4	16.5	23.6	91.0
1980	21.6	112.0	110.6	16.1	23.3	87.2
1981	20.9	114.9	110.6	15.8	22.9	84.6(c)
1982	19.3	90.1	84.1	12.7	18.2	70.1(d)
1983	20.0	92.8	86.6	12.5	18.2	74.0(d)

Sources and Notes:
(1) and (2) Banco Central de Chile, "Cuentas Nacionales de Chile: 1960-1983". Departamento de Publicaciones, Santiago, Diciembre 1984.
(3) INE, "Indices de Produccion de Industrias Manufactureras". Santiago: Division de Estadisticas Economicas, 1984.
(4) INE, "Encuesta Nacional de Empleo". Total Pais: Division de Estadisticas Economicas, various years. (a) Average 1970-1971.
(5) INE, "Encuesta Nacional de Empleo". Gran Santiago: Division de Estadisticas Economicas, various years. (b) Average 1965-1970. In 1970 the share of industrial employment was 25.4 percent.
(6) SOFOFA, "Indice de Empleo Industrial". Santiago: Departamento de Estadisticas, various years. (c) Average January to May. (d) Estimated using the INE annual surveys. SOFOFA discontinued publishing their index in May 1981.

achieved in 1970–1971. The volume of physical industrial production also declined but these contractions are less important than those indicated by the employment index.

According to the revised national accounts figures recently published by the Central Bank, industrial output decreased by 10 percent from 1970 to 1982. (See column 2 of Table 2.1.) The National Bureau of Statistics (INE) survey also shows a decline between those years of 16 percent. (See column 3 of Table 2.1.)[4] However, it is important to note that the behavior of industrial production fluctuates during the period responding to contractions (years 1975 and 1982) and to expansions (years 1976, 1977, 1978, 1979, and 1980). The Central Bank figures show a slower rate of growth in 1981 than in the previous years, only 2.6 percent compared to an average rate of 7.6 percent during the years 1975–1980. The INE and the SOFOFA figures show stagnant industrial production in 1981.

Two exogenous criteria can be used to evaluate these results. These are: (1) the historical performance of the Chilean industrial sector and (2) the performance of employment and industrial production in other Latin American and developing countries during the years 1970–1982.

According to the first criterion, we observe a sharp decline in both the rate of employment creation and industrial output during the monetarist experiment. (See Table 2.1.) Manufacturing employment was increasing at an annual average rate of 3 percent between 1967 and 1972. This same rate decreased by 2.9 percent from 1970 to 1982. During the 1960s the average annual rate of growth of manufacturing output was 5.3 percent. It decreased to −1.0 and −1.8 percent during 1970–1982 and 1974–1982, respectively. Furthermore, the share of industrial output in total GDP increased from an average of 23.8 percent between 1960 and 1965 to 25.8 percent between 1970 and 1973, in contrast with the decline during the neoconservative period.

Consequently, from an historical perspective, the role of the manufacturing sector changed drastically during the monetarist experiment. During the 1960s and early 1970s, employment and industrial output grew at relatively fast rates. This trend halted abruptly after 1974. Manufacturing industry not only lost its capability to generate new jobs, but began releasing workers to other sectors of the economy. In terms of output, after a steady increase of 5.7 percent a year from 1960 to 1972, production fell by 7.7 percent in 1973, 2.6 percent in 1974 and 25.5 percent in 1975. Output recovered the 1974 level in 1979, increased by 6.2 percent in 1980, stagnated in 1981, and fell by 21.6 percent in 1982. In 1985 industrial production was still below the 1974 level.

The other criterion used to evaluate the performance of the industrial sector involves a comparison with industrial production and employment in other countries during the same period of time. Table 2.2 shows that the rate of growth of world industrial production decreased in the second half of the 1970s. However, this rate was still relatively high, especially in the developing countries and in Latin America. The latter experienced an increase in industrial output at an average annual rate of 5.9 percent during 1969–1981 and 3.5 percent during 1974–1981. In these same periods, Chilean industrial output was practically stagnant.

A similar situation is observed with respect to industrial employment. Other Latin American countries were expanding industrial em-

TABLE 2.2 Production and Employment in the Manufacturing Sector of Developing and Latin American Countries: 1969-1981 (1975=100)

Years	Production			Employment		
	World	Developing Countries	Latin America	World	Developing Countries	Latin America
1969	78	65	64	89	70	70
1970	82	69	70	91	73	73
1971	86	75	76	92	77	75
1972	92	83	83	95	85	78
1973	101	92	93	98	90	89
1974	104	98	100	100	95	94
1975	100	100	100	100	100	100
1976	108	108	107	103	108	103
1977	114	116	112	106	113	106
1978	119	124	117	107	117	109
1979	125	128	126	108	120	112
1980	126	134	133	108	122	114
1981	127	134	127	---	---	---
Average Rate of Growth						
1969-81	4.1	6.2	5.9	1.8	5.2	4.5
1974-81	2.9	4.6	3.5	1.3	4.3	3.3

Source: United Nations, Yearbook of Industrial Statistics, 1981 edition, Vol I, 1983.

ployment at an average rate of 4.5 percent a year during 1969–1981 and 3.3 percent during 1974–1981. In Chile industrial employment was decreasing during this period. (See Table 2.2.)

Because the Chilean industrial decline was not the outcome of a generalized international pattern, nor a continuation of a historical tendency, it can be argued that this contraction was mainly the result of the particular policies followed during the monetarist experiment. As we saw in the previous chapter, the restrictive aggregate demand policies combined with the sudden openness to international trade and capital markets, produced an environment which was strongly biased against industrial development.

A second conclusion from the above figures is that the contraction of industrial production and employment was important not only in terms of magnitude, but also in terms of the duration and persistence of the phenomenon. Part of this decline showed up as lower capacity utilization rates and does not necessarily indicate changes in productive capacity. But this is just a static picture. It is logical to expect that over time the industrial structure will respond to these lower capacity utilization rates. Given the new functioning of the economy, expansions will occur in those other economic activities where demand behaves in a more dynamic way. The persistence of the structural changes not only affects capacity utilization but can eventually be expected to permanently and significantly change the structure of production.

In what follows, I attempt to analyze this issue of the loss in production capacity in the industrial sector by comparing actual production with an estimated production trend, based on historical performance. This exercise also gives an idea of the cost, in terms of industrial output and employment, of the monetarist experiment. Second, I estimate the changes occurring in productive capacity between 1969 and 1982. This estimate is done for industrial branches at a three-digit level ISIC rev. 2. Third, to support this estimate, I look at the evolution of the number of bankruptcies and the changes that occurred in the number of establishments. Fourth, I look at the impacts these changes had on the composition of manufacturing employment. Finally, the results are brought together in the last section where the main conclusions are presented.

The Reduction in Industrial Output and Employment

To approach the problem of the cost associated with the reduction in manufacturing output, it is useful to compare effective output with some measure of potential output.

In Table 2.3, column 4, two hypothetical alternatives of the evolution of industrial output are presented: one for the period 1971–1973 and another for 1974–1982. In the first period, "normal" production for the years 1971–1973 is estimated based upon the historical growth rate of industrial production during the 1960s (5.7 percent annually). In the second period (1974–1982), the estimation assumes that productive capacity was "normally" utilized in 1974.[5] Based upon this assumption the same historical growth rate (5.7 percent annually) was applied to obtain the hypothetical results for 1974–1982.

The results are presented in Table 2.3 and Diagram 2.1. They show that if industry had maintained the average annual growth rate of 5.7 percent, industrial output would have been ten billion dollars greater in 1982 than it actually was. (See Table 2.3, column 6.)[6] One can also estimate how much industrial output must grow during the next decade in order to reach a level similar to potential output by 1982. This estimate shows that industrial production would have to increase at an average annual rate of 12.1 percent, which is more than twice the growth rate of the 1960s.

This loss of dynamism is also reflected in the capacity of the industrial sector to create new jobs. If industrial output had increased

TABLE 2.3 Estimate of the Loss of Industrial Output: 1960-1982

Years	Industrial GDP (pesos 1977) (1)	Industrial GDP Annual Rate of Growth (2)	Industrial GDP (dollars 1977) (3)	Potential Industrial GDP (4)	Annual Production Losses (5)	Cumulative Production Losses (6)
1960	41,649	-	1,938.7	-	-	-
1965	55,839	4.4	2,596.8	-	-	-
1969	68,555	2.7	3,188.9	3,188.9	-	-
1970	69,912	2.0	3,252.7	3,370.7	-118.0	-118.0
1971	79,404	13.6	3,695.1	3,562.8	132.3	14.3
1972	81,180	2.2	3,776.4	3,765.9	10.5	24.8
1973	74,906	-7.7	3,485.6	3,980.5	-494.9	-470.1
1974	72,994	-2.6	3,395.0	3,395.0	0.0	0.0
1975	54,405	-25.6	2,525.9	3,588.5	1,062.6	-1,062.6
1976	57,678	6.0	2,677.4	3,793.1	-1,115.7	-2,178.3
1977	62,574	8.5	2,905.0	4,009.3	-1,104.3	-3,282.6
1978	68,374	9.3	3,175.2	4,237.8	-1,062.6	-4,345.2
1979	73,777	7.9	3,426.0	4,479.3	-1,053.3	-5,398.5
1980	78,332	6.2	3,638.5	4,734.7	-1,096.2	-6,494.7
1981	80,336	2.6	3,733.1	5,004.5	-1,271.4	-7,766.1
1982	62,983	-21.6	2,926.8	5,289.8	-2,363.0	-10,129.1

Table 2.3 (continued)

Sources and Notes:

(1) Millions of pesos of 1977. Banco Central de Chile, "Indicadores Economicos y Sociales," Departamento de Publicaciones, Santiago, 1983.

(2) Annual rate of growth of column (1).

(3) Millions of dollars of 1977. Industrial GDP in pesos of 1977 [column (1)] was divided by the average rate of 1977 (21.54 pesos = one dollar). The rest of the series was constructed using the annual growth rate calculated in column (2).

(4) Millions of dollars of 1977. Two assumptions were made to construct this series: (1) That 1969 effective output was equal to historical output and for the years 1970-1973 output grew at a rate equal to the average annual growth rate of the period 1960-1969 (5.7 percent). (2) That 1974 output was equal to historical output and during the period 1974-1982 output grew at a rate of 5.7 percent, equal to the average annual rate of the period 1960-1969.

(5) Column (3) minus column (4).

(6) Sum of column (5).

DIAGRAM 2.1. ACTUAL AND HISTORICAL PRODUCTION TREND

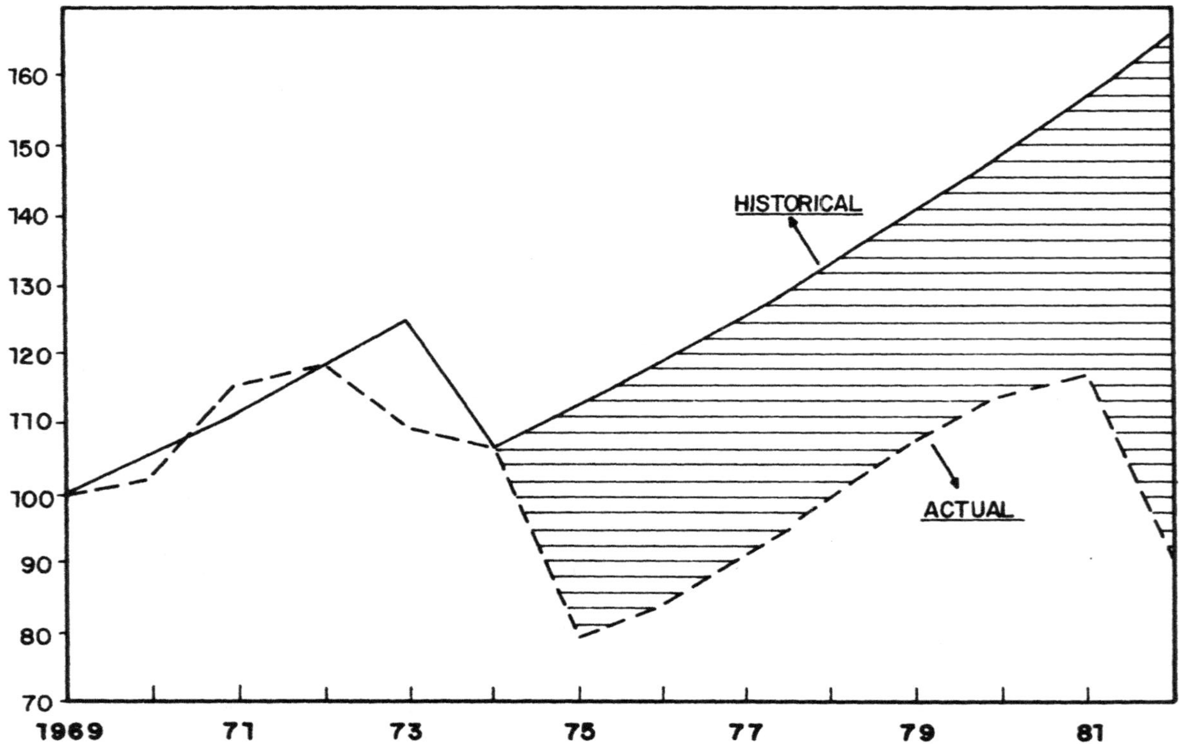

SOURCE : BASED ON DATA IN TABLE 2.3.

according to the historical rate, industrial employment would have been around 35 percent greater than it actually was in 1982. That year, approximately 15 percent of the labor force worked in the industrial sector, which means that the loss of industrial jobs increased the national unemployment rate by approximately 5 percent. This figure represents around one-fourth of the 1982 open unemployment rate.

Table 2.3 also gives an idea of the performance of the industrial sector during Allende's government (September 1970 to September 1973). If productive capacity decreased during this period, one cannot attribute industry's performance solely to policies specific to the post-September 1973 stabilization program. We must also examine the economy of the Allende years. Although the empirical evidence does not provide a clear-cut answer to this question, the following approach will help to clarify the issue.

The methodology used to construct Table 2.3, column 4, assumes that in 1974 utilizable productive capacity was 4.7 percent less than in 1971.[7] Since investment was low during 1971–1973 and some disruption occurred in the organization of the industrial sector, it seems reasonable to assume that productive capacity fell during this period. However, as stated by Ffrench-Davis (1980): ". . . the assertions that by 1973 the industrial sector was destroyed are disproved by the performance of the industrial sector immediately after the coup of September 1973: there was no general destruction; rather production stagnated." (See columns 5 and 6 of Table 2.3.) Moreover, acceptance of the actual level of industrial production in 1974 as a good representation of its "normal" level clearly underestimates the potential productive capacity for that year. The sharp reduction of aggregate demand was already underway by the second semester of 1974, with negative consequences for industrial output. This is substantiated by the fact that between October 1973 and September 1974 (the first year of the military government) industrial output was 3.4 percent greater than the 1974 average.

Furthermore, during the last years of Allende's government the economy was in a state of repressed inflation. As mentioned by Ramos (1980): ". . . the economy was in a money-abundant, goods-scarce disequilibrium, as people tried to get rid of their excessive holdings of money as soon as they could, generating instant shortages and creating black markets." This situation of excess demand for goods and repressed inflation suggests that there were no restrictions on the sale of firms, especially since part of their production could be sold at black market prices.

A detailed evaluation of the performance of the industrial sector during Allende's years goes well beyond the scope of this study. Nevertheless, particularly in 1973, the situation of political and economic instability probably reduced existent capacity albeit not in an important way. Moveover, as shown in Table 2.3, the reduction in industrial production was much greater during the military government than during Allende's time in office. Without including the 1982 recession, between the years 1975 and 1981 the loss in industrial output relative to its historical trend was on average 2.2 times greater than in 1973, the year of the military coup, and the year Chile's economic and political instability were at their worst.

The Evolution of Industrial Productive Capacity: 1969–1983

The objective of this section is to more directly estimate the performance of industrial productive capacity. This section is divided into two parts. In the first part I present the methodology which is known in the literature as the "trends through peaks" or "Wharton method." A discussion of the advantages and flaws of this method is also included. In the second part the results of the estimation are presented. However, before proceeding, it is important to clarify the meaning of some concepts that will be used here in the study.

In the literature, there are basically two theoretical definitions of capacity output (Phan-Thuy and others, 1981). On the one hand is the technical meaning of the concept. According to this definition, capacity output is the production flow associated with the input of fully utilized manpower, capital, and other relevant factors of production. In this version, there are no cost considerations nor economic limitations. Thus, capacity is measured as the maximum physical output produced per unit of time given the capital stock.

On the other hand, the economic concept of capacity output also refers to attainable levels of production over time; however, these are not necessarily the maximum levels. In this definition, all costs and constraints imposed by the linkages and interdependence among different economic sectors are taken into account. From a static microeconomic point of view, this concept assumes that if a firm is in a competitive equilibrium, capacity output is defined as the output level that a firm can produce at the minimum of the average cost curve, given the existing stock of capital, technology and factor prices.

It is not easy to distinguish between these two concepts in empirical attempts to estimate capacity output, especially when the estimates refer to an aggregate economic sector like manufacturing.[8] These problems have led to capacity output estimations which refer to potential product, defined as the maximum level of output per unit of time when all resources in the economy are fully and efficiently employed, given consumer preferences and existing technology.

As I describe below, the method used here gives estimates which are a combination of the technical and economic concept of capacity output. I use maximum historical production figures, which can be interpreted as the flow of production when all inputs are fully utilized (the technical meaning). But, the method has been adapted to consider seasonal variations, thus incorporating a demand constraint into our estimates.

In what follows, a formal presentation of the method is made together with a discussion of its advantages and flaws.

Methodology. The method used is a variation of the "trends through peaks" or "Wharton method" and can be formalized in the following way:[9]

Let $a_{i,j}$ be the production index of manufacturing group i in month j during any year of period t. Thus,

a = Production index.
i = Manufacturing groups disaggregated at three-digit ISIC.
j = January, February, March, . . . December.
t = Period of time considered for the analysis.

To adjust for seasonal variations we define Max $a_{i,j}$ as the maximum production index of group i in month j during any year of period t.

Thus, we can define the seasonal adjusted maximum capacity of production of group i during period t as:

$$m_i = \sum_j \frac{\text{Max } a_{i,j}}{12}$$

Let us define

$$w_i = \frac{VA_i}{TVA}$$

VA_i = Value added of group i.

TVA = Total industrial value added.

Thus, w_i are the value added shares of each industrial group i, in total industrial value added. They (w_i) represent the relative weights necessary to aggregate the m_i. Finally, we can define maximum capacity of production for total industry during period t as:

$$Z_t = \sum_i w_i m_i$$

The figures used are maximum values of historical production obtained from the monthly index of physical manufacturing production calculated by SOFOFA. These values do not take into account the production linkages and interdependences among manufacturing groups. It is likely that two maxima would not occur simultaneously, in which case the method would overestimate the production maximum for industry as a whole. To interpret my results, it is also important to keep in mind the differences between the concept of capacity output and the concept of maximum capacity of production. The latter refers to maximum historical production levels which, given the information available, are used in an attempt to indirectly estimate industrial capacity output. Thus, my estimates do not take into account the differences between the degrees of capacity utilization.

For example, the method used does not differentiate between maximum production levels reached with different numbers of shifts. In other words, if an industrial group in the past was able to reach a certain production level with two shifts, we assume that this same level could be reached in the future with one or three shifts. Also, the method does not correct for two maxima that cannot be reached simultaneously because they use the same inputs and equipment. If both maxima had been reached in the past, the method assumes that they could be reached simultaneously in the future. In sum, given the available information, the concept of maximum capacity of production is only an indirect approximation of the problem of measuring the evolution of capacity output in the Chilean manufacturing sector.

Furthermore, it is important to consider that my estimates refer to industrial gross output and not to industrial value added. The difference between these two concepts is that the former includes domestic and imported intermediate goods used in the production process. In a context where domestic markets were suddenly opened to international trade, these differences should be taken into account, especially in those manufacturing groups where the value added gross output ratio decreased.[10]

After these explanations defining the concepts and problems associated with the available information, I turn now to present the results of my estimation.

Analysis of the Results. Based on the observation made in the previous section, there are two points that should be considered when interpreting the results. First, the highest seasonally adjusted production level reached during a given period represents the maximum feasible output level of each manufacturing group, given its installed capacity.[11] Second, changes in the level of maximum capacity of production between two periods are proxies for changes in industrial capacity output.

The method was first applied to compare the maximum capacity of production during the years (1969–1973) with the years (1982–1983). This comparison takes into account the full impact of the monetarist experience on industrial productive capacity. As mentioned in Chapter 1, before 1982 many manufacturing firms were surviving mainly because of the great availability of loans denominated in dollars. With the devaluation in June 1982, firms' indebtedness increased in proportion with the devaluation, leading to a significant increase in the number of firms that went bankrupt.[12]

To reinforce the analysis, the method was also applied to the period (1978–1981). The objective is to compare "normal" years (1969–1973) with the period (1978–1981), which includes the "boom period," or most successful phase of the monetarist experiment.[13]

The evolution of maximum capacity output between the time periods (1969–1973) and (1982–1983) is presented in Table 2.4, columns 2, 3, 4, 5, and 6. The results show that during these 14 years, maximum production capacity in total manufacturing decreased by 9.5 percent. If we exclude the group Non-Ferrous Metal Basic Industries, the deterioration of productive capacity reached 19.2 percent.[14] (See Table 2.4, column 4.) These results are substantiated by the fact that between the two time periods (1969–1973) and (1978–1981), the latter being the best years of the monetarist experiment, productive capacity was practically stagnant, increasing by only 2.9 percent, without the group Non-Ferrous Metal Basic Industries. (See Table 2.4, column 8.)

However, to have a better idea of how these changes affected the structure of industry, it is necessary to look at the evolution of productive capacity at a more disaggregated level. The method was applied to manufacturing groups at a three-digit level and the most important results are the following:

First, out of a total of 29 groups, 23 suffered deterioration or stagnation in their productive capacity. (See Table 2.4, columns 5 and 6.) Of these 23, productive capacity remained stagnant in only six groups. The other 17 experienced a decline in their capacity.[15]

Second, manufacturing capacity declined in those groups producing the following types of goods: consumer goods like textiles, wearing apparel, leather, and footwear; durable consumer goods like machinery, communication equipment, and electrical appliances and housewares; transport equipment and intermediate goods for manufacturing like industrial chemicals, petroleum refineries, and miscellaneous products of petroleum and coal; intermediate goods for construction like pottery,

TABLE 2.4 Evolution of Maximum Capacity Output in the Chilean Manufacturing Sector: 1969-1983 (1969=100)

Major Groups	Value Added (%) (1)	Max. Cap. Output 1969-1973 (2)	Max. Cap. Output 1982-1983 (3)	(3) --- (2) (%) (4)	Deteriorated Groups (5)	Stagnant Groups (6)	Max. Cap. Output 1978-1981 (7)	(7) --- (2) (%) (8)
A. Regular Consumer Goods								
Food	16.3	118.4	129.6	109.5		x	139.0	117.4
Beverage	5.1	132.2	147.6	111.6			166.8	126.2
Textiles	10.2	130.0	100.2	77.1	x		103.7	79.8
Wearing Apparel except Footwear	2.9	123.5	70.7	57.2	x		99.4	80.5
Leather and Products of Leather	1.1	108.5	53.8	49.6	x		86.2	79.4
Footwear	1.8	134.1	67.7	46.0	x		85.9	64.1
Other Chemical Products	4.8	134.1	132.5	98.8		x	141.8	105.7
Subtotal	42.2	125.4	116.1	92.6			127.8	101.9
B. Durable Consumer Goods								
Machinery except Electric	3.2	128.7	30.0	23.3	x		53.3	41.4
Communication Equip. & Apparatus	2.0	200.7	89.4	44.5	x		201.3	100.3
Elect. Appliances & Housewares	1.8	138.4	96.7	96.9	x		263.0	190.0
Subtotal	7.0	151.8	64.1	42.2			149.5	98.5

C. Manufacture of Transport Equipment								
Transport Equipment	6.2	118.5	61.2	51.6	x		117.6	99.2
Subtotal	6.2	118.5	61.2	51.6			117.6	99.2
D. Intermediate Goods for Manufacturing								
Industrial Chemical	2.7	123.1	47.8	38.8	x		75.9	61.7
Petroleum Refineries	1.6	137.6	108.8	79.1	x		137.9	100.2
Misc. Petroleum & Coal	0.2	135.0	88.1	65.3	x		98.9	73.3
Iron & Steel Basic Industries	3.4	115.3	93.3	80.9		x	107.9	93.6
Non-Ferrous Metal Industries	13.1	130.9	201.1	153.6			197.8	151.6
Subtotal	21.0	127.9	155.8	121.8			162.1	126.7
E. Intermediate Goods for Construction								
Wood & Cork except Furniture	3.0	155.5	172.4	110.9			220.0	141.5
Furniture and Fixtures	1.0	140.8	127.5	90.6		x	223.5	158.7
Pottery, China & Earthenware	0.5	117.7	34.5	29.3	x		104.8	89.0
Glass and Glass Products	0.8	140.3	126.4	90.1		x	177.5	126.5
Other Non-Metallic Products	1.9	118.5	75.5	63.7	x		123.2	104.0
Fabricated Metal Products	4.3	126.8	74.2	58.5	x		112.8	89.0
Elect. Industrial Machinery	1.0	132.5	146.2	110.3			291.1	219.0
Subtotal	12.5	134.5	109.7	81.6			167.5	124.2

(continued)

Table 2.4 (continued)

Major Groups	Value Added (%) (1)	Max. Cap. Output 1969-1973 (2)	Max. Cap. Output 1982-1983 (3)	(3) --- (2) (%) (4)	Deteriorated Groups (5)	Stagnant Groups (6)	Max. Cap. Output 1978-1981 (7)	(7) --- (2) (%) (8)
F. Miscellaneous Manufacturing Goods								
Paper and Paper Products	2.1	107.2	122.9	114.6			129.1	120.4
Printing and Publishing	2.7	156.3	96.5	61.7	x		117.8	75.4
Rubber Products	1.6	144.7	92.8	64.1	x		114.9	79.4
Plastic Products	1.3	127.9	103.2	80.7		x	126.1	98.6
Professional Equipment	0.2	114.5	42.2	36.9	x		62.1	54.2
Other Manufacturing Industries	3.2	125.9	163.4	129.8			163.7	130.0
Subtotal	11.1	132.5	120.1	90.6			132.7	100.2
Total Manufacturing	100.0	129.3	117.0	90.5			141.3	109.3
Total Manufacturing w/o group 372	100.0	129.1	104.3	80.8			132.8	102.9

Sources: The figures used in this estimation were taken from the SOFOFA production index (1969=100).

Notes: Column (5): Groups that had a Maximum Capacity Output during 1982-1983 less than or equal to 80 percent of the Maximum Capacity Output during 1969-1973.

Column (6): Groups that had a Maximum Capacity Output during 1982-1983 greater than 80 percent and less than 110 percent of the Maximum Capacity Output during 1969-1973.

china and earthenware, non-metallic mineral products, and fabricated metal products; and miscellaneous manufactured goods like printing and publishing materials, rubber products, and professional and scientific equipment. (See Table 2.4, column 5.)

Third, productive capacity remained stagnant in those groups producing food, other chemical products, iron and steel basic industries, furniture and fixtures, glass and glass products, and plastic products. (See Table 2.4, column 6.)

Fourth, industrial capacity output increased in six cases: beverages, non-ferrous metal basic industries, wood and cork products, paper and paper products, other manufacturing industries, and electrical industrial machinery. In this last group however, there is evidence of an important reduction in its vertical integration process. As we will show in Chapter 3, the number of intermediate imported goods increased substantially in this group.

To explain this decline in the nation's manufacturing base, it is important to consider the different ways the monetarist experiment policies affected the industrial structure. Within the context of restrictive monetary and fiscal policies, the sudden openness to international trade, high interest rates, and an overvalued exchange rate, very few manufacturing groups were able to respond to the challenge of the model, which was basically to increase exports. In fact, according to the evidence presented in Table 2.4, the few groups that increased productive capacity were associated with the production of strategic exportable goods that were natural resource intensive, like non-ferrous metal basic industries which includes copper refining, wood and cork products, and paper and paper products. Another group that increased capacity output was electrical industrial machinery and apparatus, which is associated with the production of inputs for non-tradable goods generating little value added and using a high proportion of imported inputs.

The rest of the manufacturing groups were all negatively affected in their productive capacity. Especially hard hit were those groups producing non-durable and durable consumer goods that compete with imports. Also hurt were those linked to non-tradable economic activities affected by restrictions in domestic demand.[16]

Undoubtedly the other factor explaining the poor performance of industrial capacity was the low rate of investment which can be observed during the whole period. This issue will be analyzed in detail in the section titled "Changes in Productivity and Investments" in this chapter.

TABLE 2.5 Annual Number of Bankrupt Firms

Year	Number of Firms
1965	203
1966	190
1967	230
1968	229
1969	218
1970	237
1971	205
1972	97
1973	25
1974	28
1975	80
1976	131
1977	224
1978	311
1979	344
1980	415
1981	431
1982	810

Source: Fiscalia Nacional de Quiebras, Departamento de Estadisticas, 1984.

The Evolution of Manufacturing Bankruptcies and Number of Establishments

The purpose of this section is to continue analyzing the decline in the nation's manufacturing base. I now approach the problem from another angle, that of looking at the numbers of bankruptcies and establishments. The analysis is also used to support the estimates of the previous section, especially in terms of the identification of those manufacturing groups which suffered a relatively larger capacity deterioration.

The section starts by looking at the number of bankruptcies classified by economic sectors. I then focus the analysis on the manufacturing sector to identify those industrial groups in which relatively more bankruptcies occurred. Finally I look at the evolution of the number of manufacturing establishments classified by industrial groups and by size.

The Evolution of Bankruptcies by Economic Sector. In Table 2.5 the total number of bankruptcies between the years 1965 and 1982 is presented.[17] These figures correspond to the total number of firms that went bankrupt in the economy in each of the previous years. We observe that during the second half of the 1960s the number of annual bankruptcies fluctuated between 190 and 230. During the first two years of the 1970s, the number of bankruptcies continued to fall within this range, declining substantially during the 1972–1974 period. In 1975 and 1976 they begin to climb again, thereafter exceeding significantly what can historically be considered the normal number of bankruptcies. In fact, bankruptcies increased from 224 in 1977, a number comparable to what occurred during the 1960s, to 810 in 1982. Compared to 1967, the worst year of the 1960s, the number of bankrupt firms during 1982 more than tripled. Between 1965 and 1969 the average annual number of bankruptcies was 214 firms; during 1978–1982 this average increased to 462, more than doubling what had been historically observed. In other words, during the time called the "boom" (1978–1981), the number of firms going bankrupt was two times greater than in "non-boom" periods like 1965–1970.

The other issue that Table 2.5 calls attention to is the extraordinary increase in the number of bankruptcies in 1982. That year 810 firms went broke, equalling the sum total of bankruptcies in 1980 and 1981. This was especially severe in light of the fact that 1980 and 1981 witnessed a bankruptcy rate much greater than the historical average.

As mentioned before, in 1982 the economy experienced one of the worst recessions of the century. Nonetheless, 1975 was also a recessionary year, but only 80 bankruptcies occurred.[18] Undoubtedly, the extraordinarily high number of bankruptcies was a distinctive characteristic of the 1982 recession and is an important fact that must be emphasized. Before 1982 the general pattern of industrial performance could be described as an increasing accumulation of tension which finally exploded in June of 1982, when the economic authorities decided that they could no longer sustain the fixed exchange rate policy in effect since June of 1979.

During the monetarist experiment manufacturing firms used all the available mechanisms to survive in an environment that was increasingly hostile to them. As I will show in Chapter 3, one of these survival mechanisms was to go into debt. However, their debt increased to untenable levels. By the end of the second quarter of 1982 the tension reached its peak, exploding in June 1982. There were no more loans available; the firms' debt had increased overnight by an amount equal to the percentage of the devaluation. Their main life preserver disintegrated, dramatically affecting the nation's manufacturing base.

Industrial GDP declined 21.0 percent in 1982. Between the last quarters of 1981 and 1982 alone, manufacturing employment decreased by more than 140,000 employees. Additionally, the government had to intervene on behalf of the major banks to avoid the bankruptcy of the entire financial system. The ownership of the most important manufacturing firms was threatened.

I turn now to analyze the composition of bankruptcies by sectors of economic activity.[19] The figures are presented in Tables 2.6 and 2.7. They show that since 1965 bankruptcies have been concentrated in two sectors: (1) manufacturing and (2) wholesale and retail trade, restaurants and hotels. This can be clearly seen in Table 2.7 where the share of these two sectors in total bankruptcies is presented. The figures show that this indicator has declined over time. In the second half of the 1960s around 90 percent of bankruptcies occurred in these activities; between 1978 and 1982 this same percentage decreased to an average of 59.2 percent. In Table 2.6 we observe that this decline is the result of an increase in the number of bankruptcies occurring in agriculture, construction, transport, financing, and services.

Compared with the years 1965–1970 the composition of bankruptcies has changed substantially. The most important changes have occurred in the manufacturing and wholesale, retail trade sectors. Particularly important is the fact that the industrial sector increased its share in total bankruptcies from an average of 8.4 percent during 1965–1970 to 24.6 percent during 1974–1982. Between these same periods, wholesale and retail trade bankruptcies decreased their relative share from 83.8 percent to 31.1 percent. (See Table 2.7.)

This decrease is probably the result of the process of opening to international trade. With low tariffs and an overvalued exchange rate, imported goods were relatively cheaper, thus making wholesale and retail stores of imported goods more profitable. By 1980 the economy was flooded with different kinds of imported goods and an increasing number of import stores quickly appeared. In fact, by 1982 it was clear that there were too many of these stores; by 1985 many of these huge buildings constructed during the "boom" period were empty shells full of empty stores.

Three conclusions can be derived from the information presented. First, the total number of bankruptcies doubled during the monetarist experiment. Second, the largest percentage of bankruptcies occurred in the manufacturing and wholesale, retail trade activities. Third, since 1970 the largest increase in bankruptcies occurred in the manufacturing sector, with wholesale and retail trade activities substantially decreasing their share in total bankruptcies.

The Evolution of Bankruptcies in the Manufacturing Sector. The results of the previous section showed that considering the number of bankruptcies that occurred during the monetarist experiment, manufacturing activities were the most affected. The objective of this section is to broaden this analysis by looking at industrial branches disaggregated at the two-digit level. The idea is to quantify the relative impact of bankruptcies on the industrial structure, identifying those manufacturing groups that were most affected.

Table 2.8 shows that the number of bankruptcies in total manufacturing increased from an average of 19 during 1965–1970 to 76 during 1975–1982. Thus, during the monetarist experiment the number of bankruptcies occurring in manufacturing activities was four times greater than in the second half of the 1960s.

Table 2.8 also shows the available data classified by industrial groups. Table 2.9 presents the composition of manufacturing bankruptcies between the years 1965 and 1982. From this evidence it is possible to conclude that on average since 1974, 72.3 percent of total bankruptcies have occurred in three groups: textiles, wearing apparel and leather; fabricated metal products, machinery and equipment; and food, beverage and tobacco. Among these three groups the first one alone accounts for more than one-third of total bankruptcies during 1974–1982. Compared with what occurred during the 1960s, the conclusion is practically the same. These three groups account for the greater part of the increase in industrial bankruptcies, especially textiles, wearing apparel and leather.

Unfortunately, more highly disaggregated data were not available. However, the principal conclusions of this section are very similar to those reached before. The policies applied during the neoconservative experiment affected the productive capacity of the industrial sector, especially in the manufacturing of textiles, wearing apparel and leather industries and in the manufacture of fabricated metal products, machinery and equipment. (See the section titled "Analysis of the Results" in this chapter.)

The Evolution of the Number of Establishments. This section approaches the problem of quantifying the degree of industrial capacity deterioration by looking at the evolution of the number of establishments between 1967 and 1982.

The figures were taken from the Fourth and Fifth National Manufacturing Censuses, years 1967 and 1979 respectively. For the years 1980, 1981 and 1982 the Annual Manufacturing Surveys were used. Other years could not be included because the information would not be compatible.

Table 2.10 presents the basic information classified by size (10–49 and 50 or more employees) and by major manufacturing groups. Table 2.11 summarizes the most important changes that occurred in the number of establishments between 1967 and 1982.

The results for total manufacturing show that the number of establishments decreased from 6,350 in 1967 to 4,484 in 1982, i.e. a decline of 29.4 percent. However, this decline is concentrated in the last years of this period. During 1967–1979, the number of establishments fell by

TABLE 2.6 Bankruptcies by Sectors of Economic Activities, 1965-1982

Economic Sectors	1965	1966	1967	1968	1969	1970	1971	1972	1973	1974	1975	1976	1977	1978	1979	1980	1981	1982
Agriculture	1	4	3	8	5	9	2	2	-	1	1	1	10	12	14	18	33	50
Mining and Quarrying	1	1	-	-	-	1	-	1	-	-	-	-	1	5	-	-	1	6
Manufacturing	9	13	15	29	20	25	15	6	3	9	22	32	62	78	78	82	101	150
Electricity, Gas and Water	-	-	-	-	-	-	-	-	-	-	-	1	-	-	1	-	-	-
Construction	3	3	-	-	-	3	8	2	3	-	1	3	19	21	7	10	10	68
Wholesale and Retail Trade and Restaurants and Hotels	182	167	204	184	183	171	149	76	15	-	3	61	96	128	134	145	150	295
Transport, Storage and Communication	1	1	2	1	2	2	4	4	1	-	-	6	2	9	13	14	24	30

Financing, Insurance, Real Estate and Business Services	-	-	1	-	-	-	1	-	1	-	1	1	13	8	6	5	11	69
Community, Social and Personal Services	3	-	2	2	5	3	2	4	-	-	2	5	5	15	12	11	6	17
Not Adequately Defined	2	1	3	5	3	3	1	-	-	-	1	2	9	3	6	4	1	14
Without Information to Classify	1	-	-	-	-	20	23	2	2	18	49	19	7	32	73	126	94	111
Total	203	190	230	229	218	237	205	97	25	28	80	131	224	311	344	415	431	810

Source: Fiscalia Nacional de Quiebras, Departamento de Estadisticas.

TABLE 2.7 Relative Share of Manufacturing and Wholesale and Retail Trade, Restaurants and Hotels in Total Bankruptcies (Percentages), 1965-1982

	1965	1966	1967	1968	1969	1970	1971	1972	1973	1974	1975	1976	1977	1978	1979	1980	1981	1982
Manufacturing	4.4	6.8	6.5	12.7	9.2	10.5	7.3	6.2	12.0	32.1	27.5	24.4	27.7	25.1	22.7	19.8	23.4	18.5
Wholesale and Retail Trade; Restaurants and Hotels	89.7	87.9	88.7	80.3	83.9	72.2	72.7	78.4	60.0	0.0	3.8	46.6	42.9	41.2	39.0	34.9	34.8	36.4
Total	94.1	94.7	95.2	93.0	93.1	82.7	80.0	84.6	72.0	32.1	31.3	71.0	70.6	66.3	61.7	54.7	58.2	54.9

Source: Derived from data in Table 2.6.

TABLE 2.8 Manufacturing Bankruptcies, 1965-1982 (Number of Firms)

Groups	1965	1966	1967	1968	1969	1970	1971	1972	1973	1974	1975	1976	1977	1978	1979	1980	1981	1982
Food, Beverage and Tobacco	2	-	1	3	2	2	2	-	1	-	2	7	10	15	15	8	22	19
Textile, Wearing Apparel & Leather	1	3	2	5	5	7	3	2	1	4	15	13	22	24	26	37	32	53
Wood & Furniture	1	5	2	9	2	7	3	-	-	2	2	3	6	14	8	4	7	8
Paper, Printing and Publishing	-	-	1	-	-	-	2	1	-	-	-	-	1	-	3	6	6	14
Chemicals, Coal, Petroleum, Rubber & Plastic Products	1	-	-	-	2	-	1	-	-	-	1	1	4	4	9	6	7	25
Non-Metallic Mineral Products	1	-	-	-	-	-	-	-	-	-	-	-	2	2	2	3	1	10
Basic Metal Industries	-	2	1	2	2	-	-	-	1	-	1	1	7	3	1	6	9	1
Fabricated Metal Products, Machinery and Equipment	1	-	1	1	3	3	4	3	-	3	1	7	10	15	11	12	16	19
Other Manufacturing Industries	2	3	7	9	4	6	-	-	-	-	-	-	-	1	3	-	1	1
Total	9	13	15	29	20	25	15	6	3	9	22	32	62	78	78	82	101	150

Source: Fiscalia Nacional de Quiebras.

TABLE 2.9 Composition of Manufacturing Bankruptcies, 1965-1982 (Percentages)

Groups	1965	1966	1967	1968	1969	1970	1971	1972	1973	1974	1975	1976	1977	1978	1979	1980	1981	1982
Food, Beverage and Tobacco	22.2	-	6.7	10.3	10.0	8.0	13.3	-	33.3	-	9.1	21.9	16.1	19.2	19.2	9.8	21.8	12.7
Textile, Wearing Apparel & Leather	11.1	23.1	13.3	17.2	25.0	28.0	20.0	33.3	33.3	44.4	68.2	40.6	35.5	30.8	37.3	45.1	31.7	35.3
Wood & Furniture,	11.1	38.5	13.3	31.0	10.0	28.0	20.0	-	-	22.2	9.1	9.4	9.7	17.9	10.3	4.9	6.9	5.3
Paper, Printing and Publishing	-	-	6.7	-	-	-	13.3	16.7	-	-	-	-	1.6	-	3.8	7.3	5.9	9.3
Chemicals, Coal, Petroleum, Rubber & Plastic Products	11.1	-	-	-	10.0	-	6.7	-	-	-	4.5	3.1	6.5	5.1	11.5	7.3	6.9	16.7
Non-Metallic Mineral Products	11.1	-	-	-	-	-	-	-	-	-	-	-	3.2	2.6	2.6	3.7	1.0	6.7
Basic Metal Industries	-	15.4	6.7	6.9	10.0	-	-	-	33.3	-	4.5	3.1	11.3	3.8	1.3	7.3	8.9	0.7
Fabricated Metal Products, Machinery and Equipment	11.1	-	6.7	3.4	15.0	12.0	26.7	50.0	-	33.3	4.5	21.9	16.1	19.2	14.1	14.6	15.8	12.7
Other Manufacturing Industries	22.2	23.1	46.7	31.0	20.0	24.0	-	-	-	-	-	-	-	1.3	3.8	-	1.0	0.7
Total	100	100	100	100	100	100	100	100	100	100	100	100	100	100	100	100	100	100

Source: Derived from data in Table 2.8.

only 8.5 percent, while during 1979–1982 this same percentage was 22.9 percent. Excluding the wood and cork group,[20] the results show a decline of 21.8 percent between 1967 and 1982, remaining stagnant between 1967 and 1979 and dropping by 21.9 percent between 1979 and 1982. (See Table 2.11.) Thus, our first conclusion is that the number of manufacturing establishments decreased significantly during the neo-conservative experiment.

Table 2.11 also shows those manufacturing groups which experienced a decline in number of establishments greater than the total industry average during the 1967–1982 period. They are groups producing regular consumer goods like beverages, textiles, wearing apparel, leather, and footwear.

Also included are groups producing intermediate goods for construction, like wood and cork, furniture, glass, other non-metallic mineral products, fabricated metal products, and electrical industrial machinery and apparatus. Finally, there are groups producing durable consumer goods, like machinery, communication equipment, and electrical appliances and groups producing intermediate goods for manufacturing, like iron and steel basic industries, and groups producing transport equipment and professional and scientific equipment. All of these, with the exception of beverages, wood and cork, machinery, and professional and scientific equipment, experienced a much larger decline during 1979–1982 than between 1967 and 1979.

In order to evaluate whether this decline in the number of industrial establishments was the result of a concentration process in bigger firms, the figures were classified by size (10–49 and 50 and more employees).[21] The results for total manufacturing show that the bigger firms (50 and more employees) experienced a larger decline than the smaller ones (10–49 employees). This process was especially strong in some industrial groups like textiles, glass, and machinery. Other groups like leather, footwear, furniture, electric machinery apparatus, transport equipment, and professional and scientific equipment also experienced a decrease in the larger firm category, but only during the 1967–1979 period. This suggests that after 1979 the smaller firms were relatively more affected.[22]

A possible explanation for these facts is related to the different characteristics and the ways firms operated during the monetarist experiment. Smaller firms operate with a higher percentage of family members; their production is mostly for the domestic markets and they have little or no access to the financial market. These characteristics explain why they were relatively less affected by the loss in international competitiveness and the high interest rates. On the other hand, the bigger establishments were affected by competition with imported goods and the loss in competitiveness of exports. They also had greater access

TABLE 2.10 Number of Manufacturing Establishments: 1967-1982

Major Groups	10 - 49 Employees					50 or More Employees					Total				
	1967	1979	1980	1981	1982	1967	1979	1980	1981	1982	1967	1979	1980	1981	1982
Food	1,162	1,342	1,258	1,188	1,169	212	268	249	233	214	1,374	1,610	1,507	1,421	1,383
Beverage	289	137	122	92	90	86	74	66	66	61	375	211	188	158	151
Tobacco	1	1	1	1	1	3	2	3	3	3	4	3	4	4	4
Textiles	397	378	340	303	282	170	125	105	100	68	567	503	445	403	350
Wearing Apparel	314	353	304	265	239	71	88	94	81	66	385	441	398	346	305
Leather	82	75	63	52	43	24	15	13	16	16	106	90	76	68	59
Footwear	166	148	122	104	98	56	37	34	33	29	222	185	156	137	127
Wood and Cork	963	416	337	320	294	105	108	112	86	64	1,068	524	449	406	354
Furniture	185	193	170	149	122	28	18	22	22	21	213	211	192	171	143
Paper	54	48	48	38	35	19	22	19	22	21	73	70	67	60	56
Printing and Publishing	162	196	179	165	158	42	47	48	41	38	204	243	227	206	196
Indust. Chemicals	56	50	39	42	41	22	15	20	17	15	78	65	59	59	56
Other Chemicals	115	99	95	89	81	61	72	72	70	67	176	171	167	159	148
Petrol. Refineries	6	4	5	6	5	6	6	4	3	4	12	10	9	9	9
Misc. Petroleum and Coal	3	5	4	6	6	2	3	3	3	3	5	8	7	9	9
Rubber Products	27	48	52	46	41	13	15	14	13	12	40	63	66	59	53
Plastic Products	68	134	131	113	112	25	36	32	36	30	93	170	163	149	142
Pottery, China and Earthenware	12	8	8	8	12	3	5	5	2	3	15	13	13	10	15

Glass	17	18	17	18	17	23	15	11	11	7	40	33	28	29	24
Other Non-Metallic Minerals	119	104	106	93	85	29	31	33	35	25	148	135	139	128	110
Non-Ferrous Metal Ind.	10	18	14	10	12	16	16	17	18	15	26	34	31	28	27
Metal Products	362	346	331	303	277	100	113	116	110	88	462	459	447	413	365
Iron & Steel Basic	34	41	28	26	18	19	23	20	16	17	53	64	48	42	35
Elect. Machinery	49	52	38	35	33	37	35	34	29	24	86	87	72	64	57
Transport Equip.	109	111	88	77	69	63	39	36	35	25	172	150	124	112	94
Professional and Scientific Equip.	17	12	15	10	11	5	3	5	4	4	22	15	20	14	15
Other Industries	75	66	57	53	51	18	11	9	10	4	93	77	66	63	55
Total	5,023	4,524	4,071	3,710	3,509	1,327	1,289	1,237	1,162	975	6,350	5,813	5,308	4,872	4,484
Total without Wood and Cork	4,060	4,108	3,734	3,390	3,215	1,222	1,181	1,125	1,076	911	5,282	5,289	4,859	4,466	4,130

Sources:
1967 and 1979: INE, IV and V Censo Nacional Manufacturero; Santiago: Division de Estadisticas Industriales.
1980, 1981 and 1982: INE, Encuestas Manufactureras Anuales; Santiago: Division de Estadisticas Industriales.

TABLE 2.11 Changes in the Number of Manufacturing Establishments, 1967-1982 (Percentages)

	10-49	50 or More	Total	10-49	50 or More	Total	10-49	50 or More	Total
1) Total Manufacturing									
a) With Wood and Cork	-30.1	-26.5	-29.4	-9.9	-2.9	-8.5	-22.4	-24.4	-22.9
b) Without Wood and Cork	-20.8	-25.5	-21.8	1.8	-3.4	0.1	-21.7	-22.9	-21.9
2) Groups with Largest Decline									
Beverage	-68.9	-29.1	-59.7	-52.6	-14.0	-43.7	-34.3	-17.6	-28.4
Textiles	-29.0	-60.0	-38.3	-4.8	-26.5	-11.3	-25.4	-45.6	-30.4
Wearing Apparel	-23.9	-7.0	-20.8	12.4	23.9	14.5	-32.3	-25.0	-30.8
Leather	-47.6	-33.3	-44.3	-8.5	-37.5	-15.1	-42.7	6.7	-34.4
Footwear	-41.0	-48.2	-42.8	-10.8	-33.9	-16.7	-33.8	-21.6	-31.4
Wood and Cork	-69.5	-39.0	-66.9	-56.8	2.9	-50.9	-29.3	-40.7	-32.4
Furniture	-34.1	-25.0	-32.9	4.3	-35.7	-0.9	-36.8	16.7	-32.2
Glass	0.0	-69.6	-40.0	5.9	34.8	-17.5	-5.6	-53.3	-27.3
Other Non-Metallic Mineral Products	-28.6	-13.8	-25.7	-12.6	6.9	-8.8	-18.3	-19.4	-18.5
Iron and Steel Basic Industries	-47.1	-10.5	-34.0	20.6	21.1	20.8	-56.1	-26.1	-45.3
Fabricated Metal Products	-23.5	-12.0	-21.0	-4.4	13.0	-0.6	-19.9	-22.1	-20.5
Machinery	-36.7	-55.1	-42.0	-28.4	31.9	-29.4	-11.6	-34.0	-17.9
Electrical Machinery Apparatus	-32.7	-35.1	-33.7	6.1	-5.4	1.2	-36.5	-31.4	-34.5
Transport Equipment	-36.7	-60.3	-45.3	1.8	-38.1	-12.8	-37.8	-35.9	-37.3
Professional & Scientific Equip.	-35.3	-20.0	-31.8	-29.4	-40.0	-31.8	-8.3	33.3	0.0

Source: Derived from data in Table 2.10.

to international and domestic credit, but, as we will see later in Chapter 3, at interest rates that made it impossible for them to repay those loans, at least in the short run.

The Composition of Manufacturing Employment

The results of the first section of this chapter showed that during the neoconservative experiment the manufacturing sector lost its capacity to generate employment. The main conclusion of that section was that between 1974 and 1982 there was an absolute reduction in the number of manufacturing jobs.

The purpose of this section is to broaden this analysis by looking at employment figures for the different manufacturing groups. The objective is to determine the changes that occurred in the structure of industrial employment over time. The main reason for this analysis is to assess the effects of deindustrialization on the capacity of the economy to create new jobs. The deterioration of industrial capacity not only destroys manufacturing jobs that are not replaced in other economic activities, but also introduces supply rigidities, reducing the possibilities of increasing output and employment in the future. In the short run, expansion of demand could induce severe bottlenecks, especially in those manufacturing groups that have been most affected by reductions in productive capacity. In the long run, investment becomes the main determinant of employment and output growth. However, in an economy with severe external debt problems, foreign exchange (to import the necessary equipment to increase productive capacity) becomes the most scarce resource in the economy.

Undoubtedly, the manufacturing sector has to recover its capacity to create new jobs, in order to bring down the extraordinarily high unemployment rate that has persisted since 1974. Nonetheless, to determine to what extent this recovery is possible, we first need to have a clearer assessment of the changes that occurred in the industrial sector. Particularly important seems to be the evolution of employment among manufacturing groups.

Another objective of this section is to analyze to what extent the decline of productive capacity, the reduction of the number of establishments, and the increase in bankruptcies affected manufacturing employment and in what manufacturing groups. Thus, the results obtained in this section will also be useful in supporting the conclusions of the previous sections.

A final note should be made before looking at the figures. All the data used in this section come from the fourth and fifth national manufacturing censuses and the annual manufacturing surveys done by the National Bureau of Statistics (INE). In terms of coverage and quality, these sources are probably the best figures available.[23]

The raw data are presented in Table 2.12 and the most important changes are summarized in Table 2.13. There we observe that between 1967 and 1982 the drop in manufacturing employment reached the stunning figure of 31.8 percent, which means that employment was decreasing at an average annual rate of 2.5 percent. Breaking down that period of time into (1967–1979) and (1979–1982), the results show that in the former, employment decreased by 5.2 percent, while in the latter this percentage was 28.0 percent.[24] This means that between 1979 and 1982 employment was decreasing at an average annual rate of 10.4 percent.

Unfortunately, there are no figures for the individual years in between (i.e., 1968–1978) for total manufacturing. Comparable employment data is only available for the 1967–1982 period for firms employing more than 50 workers. The figures are presented in Table 2.14 in order to give an idea of the trend in manufacturing employment. We observe that between 1967 and 1973, industrial employment was increasing at an average annual rate of 2.1 percent. Only in 1969 did employment fall between those years. During the monetarist experiment (1974–1982) industrial employment fell every year at an annual rate of 6.2 percent with 1977 being the only exception.

It is interesting to note that during the 1982 recession the reduction in manufacturing employment was much greater than in the 1975 recession (−7.0 percent versus −20.8 percent—see Table 2.14). In spite of the fact that industrial GDP declined more in 1975 than in 1982 (25.5 percent versus 21.0 percent), entrepreneurs' expectations for a rapid recovery after 1975 were high; thus, the short-run employment/output elasticity was relatively low during that recession.

On the other hand, the 1982 recession was the result of the accumulation of tensions and disequilibrium that abruptly exploded in the second semester of that year. Most firms and banks were technically bankrupt and the country had an external debt almost equal to the flow of goods and services produced in a year. Apparently, entrepreneurs perceived the 1982 recession as the "end of the road" and thus the impact on employment was relatively much stronger, making the employment/output elasticity greater than minus one during that recession.

I turn now to analyze the evolution of employment among manufacturing groups. First, it is important to notice that during 1967–1982, out of a total of 28 groups, employment increased in only five groups: food (4.6 percent), paper (3.1 percent), miscellaneous products from petroleum and coal (45.1 percent), plastic products (7.2 percent), and non-ferrous metal basic industries (38.1 percent).

TABLE 2.12 Manufacturing Employment: 1967-1982

Major Groups	10 - 49 Employees					50 or More Employees				
	1967	1979	1980	1981	1982	1967	1979	1980	1981	1982
Food	22,687	25,608	24,442	23,308	23,021	30,591	41,659	40,457	38,379	32,692
Beverage	4,257	2,905	2,634	1,969	1,935	7,062	9,041	8,373	7,972	7,288
Tobacco	20	15	12	14	11	1,481	986	1,103	1,096	782
Textiles	9,125	8,542	6,894	6,185	5,757	37,353	28,062	22,612	19,782	13,132
Wearing Apparel	6,324	6,970	6,187	5,441	4,868	10,052	12,279	11,819	10,474	7,786
Leather	1,878	1,512	1,264	1,083	854	2,763	1,831	1,634	1,802	1,615
Footwear	3,247	2,938	2,537	2,271	2,167	9,663	6,299	5,853	5,473	4,642
Wood and Cork	10,615	8,812	6,969	6,921	5,836	12,960	14,927	14,541	12,084	7,595
Furniture	3,485	3,457	3,238	2,888	2,333	3,307	2,279	2,542	2,629	2,146
Paper	1,107	921	1,002	864	737	4,475	5,962	6,020	6,201	5,019
Printing and Publishing	3,271	3,736	3,327	3,053	2,796	6,724	7,993	7,975	7,576	6,984
Industrial Chemicals	1,400	954	755	869	850	4,120	2,566	2,418	1,750	1,514
Other Chemicals Products	2,570	2,114	2,081	2,062	1,757	9,400	11,286	10,820	10,745	10,076
Petroleum Refineries	227	66	110	140	110	1,793	1,945	1,751	1,659	1,369
Misc. Petroleum & Coal	83	106	95	137	130	272	349	401	400	385
Rubber Products	530	1,057	1,260	1,069	870	3,204	3,600	3,480	3,048	2,239
Plastic Products	1,644	2,706	2,758	2,515	2,366	3,562	4,423	3,751	4,321	3,213
Pottery, China & Earthenware	263	146	116	118	163	2,245	2,052	1,505	339	731

(continued)

Table 2.12 (continued)

Major Groups	10 - 49 Employees					50 or More Employees				
	1967	1979	1980	1981	1982	1967	1979	1980	1981	1982
Glass	282	377	411	464	418	4,477	2,776	2,028	1,682	963
Other Non-Metallic Minerals	2,360	1,989	2,086	1,849	1,639	5,052	4,616	4,857	5,039	3,510
Iron & Steel Basic Ind.	839	1,017	764	703	477	10,247	9,430	8,074	6,593	6,402
Non-Ferrous Metal Ind.	234	355	315	220	219	5,608	7,282	9,104	8,510	7,849
Fabricated Metal Products	7,829	6,892	7,050	6,507	5,692	15,734	14,404	14,272	12,886	10,928
Machinery	3,844	2,561	2,093	2,209	2,262	12,147	7,382	8,120	10,468	6,493
Electrical Machinery Apparatus	1,097	1,055	817	802	762	6,882	6,584	5,611	4,715	2,975
Transport Equipment	2,341	2,348	1,836	1,575	1,421	19,933	8,015	7,064	5,738	3,618
Prof. & Scientif. Equip.	524	245	321	228	247	496	271	449	338	266
Other Manufacturing Ind.	1,385	1,295	1,043	1,009	954	1,955	1,117	886	932	274
Total	93,468	90,699	82,417	76,473	70,652	233.545	219,416	207,520	192,631	152,486

Table 2.12 (continued)

Major Groups	Total Employment				
	1967	1979	1980	1981	1982
Food	53,278	67,267	64,899	61,687	55,713
Beverage	11,319	11,946	11,007	9,941	9,223
Tobacco	1,501	1,001	1,115	1,110	793
Textiles	46,478	36,604	29,506	25,967	18,889
Wearing Apparel	16,376	19,249	18,006	15,915	12,654
Leather	4,641	3.343	2,898	2,885	2,469
Footwear	12,910	9,237	8,390	7,744	6,809
Wood and Cork	23,575	23,739	21,510	19,005	13,431
Furniture	6,792	5,736	5,780	5,517	4,479
Paper	5,582	6,883	7,022	7,065	5,756
Printing and Publishing	9,995	11,729	11,302	10,629	9,780
Industrial Chemicals	5,520	3,520	3,173	2,619	2,364
Other Chemicals Products	11,970	13,400	12,901	12,807	11,833
Petroleum Refineries	2,020	2,011	1,861	1,799	1,479
Misc. Petroleum & Coal	355	455	496	537	515
Rubber Products	3,734	4,657	4,740	4,117	3,109
Plastic Products	5,206	7,129	6,509	6,836	5,579
Pottery, China & Earthenware	2,508	2,198	1,621	457	894
Glass	4,759	3,153	2,439	2,146	1,381
Other Non-Metallic Minerals	7,412	6,605	6,943	6,888	5,149
Iron & Steel Basic Ind.	11,086	10,447	8,838	7,296	6,879
Non-Ferrous Metal Ind.	5,842	7,637	9,419	8,730	8,068
Fabricated Metal Products	23,563	21,296	21,322	19,393	16,620
Machinery	15,991	9,943	10,213	12,677	8,755
Electrical Machinery Apparatus	7,979	7,639	6,428	5,517	3,737
Transport Equipment	22,274	10,363	8,900	7,313	5,039
Prof. & Scientif. Equip.	1,020	516	770	566	513
Other Manufact. Ind.	3,340	2,412	1,929	1,941	1,228
Total	327,013	310,115	289,937	269,104	223,138

Sources:
1967 and 1979: INE, IV and V Censo Nacional Manufacturero; Santiago: Division de Estadisticas Industriales.
1980, 1981 and 1982: INE, Encuestas Manufactureras Anuales; Santiago: Division de Estadisticas Industriales.

TABLE 2.13 Changes in Manufacturing Employment: 1967-1982 (Percentages)

	1967-1982			1979-1982		
	10-49	50 or More	Total	10-49	50 or More	Total
1) Total Manufacturing	-24.4	-34.7	-31.8	-22.1	-30.5	-28.0
2) Groups with Largest Decline						
Tobacco	-45.0	-47.2	-47.2	-26.7	-20.7	-20.8
Textiles	-36.9	-64.8	-59.4	-32.6	-53.2	-48.4
Leather	-54.5	-41.5	-46.8	-43.5	-10.9	-26.1
Footwear	-33.3	-52.0	-47.3	-26.2	-26.3	-26.3
Wood and Cork	-45.0	-41.4	-43.0	-33.8	-49.1	-43.4
Furniture	-33.1	-35.1	-34.1	-32.5	-5.8	-21.9
Industrial Chemicals	-39.3	-63.3	-57.2	-10.9	-41.0	-32.8
Pottery, China & Earthenware	-38.0	-67.4	-64.4	11.6	-64.4	-59.3
Glass	48.2	-78.5	-71.0	10.9	-65.3	-56.2
Iron and Steel Basic Indust.	-43.1	-37.5	-37.9	-53.1	-32.1	-34.2
Machinery	-41.2	-46.5	-45.3	-11.7	-12.0	-11.9
Elect. Machinery Apparatus	-30.5	-56.8	-53.2	-27.8	-54.8	-51.1
Transport Equipment	-39.3	-81.8	-77.4	-39.5	-54.9	-51.4
Prof. & Scientific Equip.	-52.9	-46.4	-49.7	0.8	-1.8	-0.6
Other Manufact. Industries	-31.1	-86.0	-63.2	-26.3	-75.5	-49.1

Source: Derived from data in Table 2.12.

TABLE 2.14 Total Employment in Manufacturing Firms with 50 or More Employees: 1967-1982

Year	Employment	Annual Change (%)
1967	233,545	-
1968	242,236	3.7
1969	237,755	-1.8
1970	244,265	2.7
1971	247,612	1.4
1972	259,710	4.9
1973	264,972	2.0
1974	254,046	4.1
1975	236,350	-7.0
1976	222,885	-5.7
1977	226,584	1.7
1978	(a)	(a)
1979	219,416	-3.2
1980	207,520	-5.4
1981	192,631	-7.2
1982	152,486	-20.8
Average Annual Rates		
1967-1982		-2.8
1967-1973		2.1
1974-1982		-6.2

Source: INE, "Encuestas Manufactureras Anuales", Santiago, Division de Estadisticas Industriales, various years.

Note: (a) No information available.

In all the other groups, employment fell rapidly; Table 2.13 presents those groups that had the greatest employment reductions (greater than the average for total manufacturing). Especially important is the decline in those groups that in 1967 employed the largest proportion of employees (textiles, wood and cork,[25] fabricated metal products, wearing apparel, and transport equipment). Moreover, the decline is also impressive in the rest of the groups, reaching more than 60 percent in some cases, like pottery, china and earthenware (−64.4 percent), glass (−71.0 percent), transport equipment (−77.4 percent), and other manufacturing industries (−63.2 percent). As analyzed in detail in Chapter 3, all of these groups were affected by a combination of restrictive aggregate demand policies, import penetration, and high interest rates.

Table 2.14 also shows the performance of manufacturing employment during the 1979–1982 period. We observe that most of the groups experienced their largest decline during this period, mirroring the pattern of total industry.

The first conclusion of this section is that important changes occurred in the composition of manufacturing employment. In particular, groups with the largest share in total employment experienced a sharp decline during the monetarist experiment. One may also conclude that our findings give support to the conclusions of the previous two sections. In fact, 11 of the 15 groups that experienced the largest decline in employment (see Table 2.13) also had the largest decline in the number of establishments. (See Table 2.11.) Comparing those groups that had relatively more bankruptcies, the same phenomenon is observed.[26]

Conclusions

The main conclusions thus far in Chapter 2 are summarized in Table 2.15 and Table 2.16. In the former the results obtained for total manufacturing are presented. We observe a very poor performance of industrial output and employment relative to historical and Latin American standards during the neoconservative experiment. (See Table 2.15, rows 1 and 2.) This decline was accompanied by sharp increases in the number of bankruptcies, reductions in the number of establishments, and severe deterioration of output capacity. (See Table 2.15, rows 3, 4 and 5.)

Table 2.16 identifies which manufacturing groups were relatively more responsible for this deindustrialization process. In this table, the conclusions of the previous sections are brought together identifying which groups were more affected by (1) reductions in employment and number of establishments (greater than the average for total manufacturing), (2) increases in the number of bankruptcies (also greater than total average), and (3) deterioration of productive capacity.[27]

Thus, if in Table 2.16 a group has four X's, it means that the group did worse than the total manufacturing average in each of the indicators mentioned above. Hence, the following groups with four X's were relatively more affected by the deindustrialization process: textiles, leather, footwear, machinery, electrical machinery, transport equipment, and scientific equipment. A severe deterioration also occurred in wearing apparel and metal products, although employment in these two groups declined at a rate less than the average for total manufacturing.

Most of these groups produce regular and durable consumer goods that compete with imports. Thus they were relatively more affected by external competition due to the sudden openness to international trade and the restriction of domestic demand. This will be the subject of the next chapter, namely, to identify the sources of structural change among manufacturing groups.

TABLE 2.15 Summary of Deindustrialization Indicators for the Chilean Manufacturing Sector: 1974-1982

	1974	1975	1976	1977	1978	1979	1980	1981	1982	Averages
1) GDP										
Developing Countries (1974=100)	100.0	102.0	110.2	118.4	126.5	130.6	136.7	136.7	-	120.1(a)
Latin America (1974=100)	100.0	100.0	107.0	112.0	117.0	126.0	133.0	127.0	-	115.3(a)
Chile (1974=100)	100.0	74.5	79.0	85.7	93.7	101.1	107.3	110.1	86.3	104.7(a)
Chile: Share of Manuf. GDP	25.1	21.5	22.0	21.7	22.0	21.9	21.6	20.9	19.3	21.8(b)
2) Employment										
Developing Countries (1974=100)	100.0	105.3	113.7	118.9	123.2	126.3	128.4	-	-	116.5(c)
Latin America (1974=100)	100.0	106.4	109.6	112.8	116.0	119.1	121.3	-	-	112.2(c)
Chile (1974=100)	100.0	90.6	83.9	83.4	83.3	82.4	79.0	76.6	63.5	86.1(c)
Chile: Share of Manuf. Employment	-	17.2	17.0	16.7	16.3	16.5	16.1	15.8	12.7	16.0(d)
3) Number of Bankruptcies										
Total	28	80	131	224	311	344	415	431	810	308(e)
Manufacturing	9	22	32	62	78	78	82	101	150	68(f)
4) Number of Establishments (1967=100)										
Total Manufacturing (g)	-	-	-	-	-	91.5	83.6	76.7	70.6	-
5) Capacity Output		Average (1969-1973)				Average (1982-1983)			Change (%)	
Total Manufacturing		129.3				117.0			-9.5	
Total without Non-Ferrous Metal Industries		129.1				104.3			-19.2	

(continued)

Table 2.15 (continued)

Sources: GDP: Table 2.1 and Table 2.2.
Bankruptcies: Table 2.5 and Table 2.6.
Number of Establishments: Table 2.11.
Capacity Output: Table 2.4.

Notes: (a) Average 1974-1981.
(b) Average 1974-1982. The average for 1970-1973 was 25.9 percent.
(c) Average 1974-1980.
(d) Average 1975-1982. The average for 1970-1971 was 21.5 percent.
(e) Average 1974-1982. The average for 1965-1973 was 182.
(f) Average 1974-1982. The average for 1965-1973 was 15.
(g) Manufacturing firms with 10 or more employees.

TABLE 2.16 Summary of Deindustrialization Indicators by Manufacturing Groups

Groups	Employment (1967-1982)	No. of Establishments (1967-1982)	Bankruptcies (1967-1982)	Capacity Output [(1969-73)-(1982-83)]
Food	-	-	-	-
Beverage	-	x	-	-
Tobacco	x	-	-	-
Textiles	x	x	x	x
Wearing Apparel	-	x	x	x
Leather	x	x	x	x
Footwear	x	x	x	x
Wood and Cork	x	x	-	-
Furniture	x	x	-	-
Paper	-	-	-	-
Printing	-	-	-	x
Chemicals	x	-	-	x
Other Chemicals	-	-	-	-
Petrol. Refineries	-	-	-	x
Misc. Petrol. & Coal	-	-	-	x
Rubber	-	-	-	x
Plastic	-	-	-	-
Pottery and China	x	-	-	x
Glass	x	x	-	-
Non-Metal. Minerals	-	x	-	x
Iron and Steel	x	x	-	-
Non-Ferrous Metal	-	-	-	-
Metal Products	-	x	x	x
Machinery	x	x	x	x
Electr. Machinery	x	x	x	x
Transport Equip.	x	x	x	x
Scientif. Equip.	x	x	x	x
Others	x	-	-	-

Sources: Employment: Table 2.13
Number of Establishments: Table 2.11
Bankruptcies: Table 2.8
Capacity Output: Table 2.4

Notes: x means that there was a decline in Employment and in The Number of Establishments greater than the average for total manufacturing, an increase in bankruptcies greater than total average, and a deterioration of productive capacity.

Efficiency and Deindustrialization

The issue of improving overall economic efficiency was undoubtedly at the heart of the neoconservative model. An interesting example of this is the notion the economic authorities had at that time about the role bankruptcies played in the economy: ". . . we cannot forget that bankruptcies are the knowledgeable way in which an economy puts a final end to an inefficient investment. In this way, productive resources are moved to more profitable activities or an inefficient management is replaced by a more efficient one."[28]

The adjustment process implicit in this notion is that in private, competitive market economies, bankruptcies are one of the adjustment mechanisms to improve the resource allocation process. Because factors of production are mobile, productivity rises when they move from relatively low profit activities to more productive and efficient ones. Thus, if a bankruptcy occurs, it is a sign that the market mechanism is working, punishing inefficiency and rewarding more productive activities.

The purpose of this section is to assess to what extent the changes occurring in the manufacturing sector should be understood as a movement towards greater efficiency. The objective is to examine whether the contraction of the sector should be interpreted as a movement in the right direction, in the sense that it was the kind of resource reallocation process pursued by the policy makers, or if it is evidence of failure of the model.

One of the foundations of the neoconservative model was opening the economy to international trade. The purpose was to take advantage of the international economy, promoting efficiency and competition through a growth process based on comparative advantages, greater specialization, and economies of scale. The argument in favor of the opening-up process had two elements: (1) the desire to transform exports into the dynamic sector of the economy and (2) the idea that increased efficiency in the industrial sector could come about via external competition.

In this section I use three criteria to assess the validity of these arguments. First, I look at the changes in the structure of employment among economic activities. If the resource reallocation process promoted by the neoconservatives was successful, the reduction of jobs in the industrial sector should have been compensated for by the creation of high-productivity jobs in non-manufacturing sectors. Second, I analyze the contribution of manufacturing to the external commercial balance. Given the foreign exchange constraint of the Chilean economy, another criterion is whether the manufacturing sector increased its ability to generate foreign exchange during the neoconservative experiment. Third, I look at the changes in productivity and investment. The objective here is to determine to what extent the reduction in industrial employment was the result of productive adjustments within the sector. Did firms respond to import competition by changing their productive structure, increasing labor productivity?

TABLE 2.17 Changes in the Structure of Employment: 1970-1981

	Percentages
1) Changes in the Composition of Employment by Economic Activities.	
Manufacturing	-56.5
Construction	-43.5
Energy	2.1
Wholesale & Retail Trade: Transport & Services	59.8
Financing	38.1
2) Changes in the Labor Market Structure (a)	
Manufacturing	-25.7
Non-Manufacturing Modern Activities	-66.6
Sub-total Modern Activities	-92.3
Informal Sector	17.9
Domestic Services	-7.7
Minimum Employment Program (b)	33.1
Open Unemployment	49.0

Source: Tokman, V. "Monetarismo Global y Destruccion Industrial," Revista CEPAL, No. 23, Agosto 1984.

Notes:
(a) The coefficients are estimated in the following way: The employment structure of the initial year (1970-71) is applied to the economically active population of the final year (1981) minus effective employment in 1981.
(b) The minimum Employment Program is a government emergency employment program where workers earn around thirty dollars a month.

The Characteristics of the New Job Openings

The figures necessary to apply the first criteria are presented in Table 2.17.[29] As concluded before, manufacturing employment de creased not only in relative terms, with respect to total employment, but also in absolute terms. Following the traditional classification by economic activities, we observe that wholesale and retail trade and services were the sectors that absorbed, in part, the decline in manufacturing and construction employment. Also, due to the expansion of capital markets, employment increased in the financial sector as well. (See Table 2.17, row 1.) However, this classification by economic activities does not permit us to evaluate the type of jobs that were generated during the monetarist experiment. Hence, a classification is needed that will enable us to identify the quality and productivity of the new jobs generated in the economy. Following the methodology developed in

PREALC (1982), the labor market may be broken down into two rural and two urban segments, distinguishing in the latter a modern and an informal sector. It is then possible to analyse the destination of those workers released by the manufacturing sector. The figures of Table 2.17, row 2 show that between the end of 1970 and 1981, out of every 26 workers released by the manufacturing sector, 13 joined the lines of the openly unemployed, five became members of the urban informal sector, and eight had to work for US$30 a month in a government emergency employment program called the minimum employment program.

Hence, the results show that the new jobs were not created in those non-manufacturing modern activities. In fact, if we consider the people working in the minimum employment program as unemployed, most of those workers released by manufacturing became unemployed and the rest became informal workers. It could still be argued, however, that the reallocation process implied that workers moved away from the urban sector into rural activities. The information available shows that this was not the case. Between 1970 and 1981, rural employment decreased in absolute terms by around 14,000 workers. Moreover, assuming a constant share of rural employment in the labor force between those years, employment in the rural sector would have been 150,000 greater than what was effectively observed in 1981.[30]

The Ability to Generate Foreign Exchange

This section presents a second criterion to assess whether the shrinkage of the manufacturing sector could be interpreted as a movement towards greater efficiency.

One of the objectives the neoconservatives had when they opened the economy to international trade was to increase exports. They believed that past protective measures were biased against exports and that the elimination of quantitative and qualitative restrictions to trade would move resources away from inefficient import substitution activities towards exports. In particular, they thought that the new policies would encourage the production of non-traditional exports, which in turn would become the main source of economic growth.

The objective of this section is to empirically assess this argument in two ways. The first is by looking at the resource reallocation process embodied in the performance of manufacturing net exports (exports minus imports). In other words, the purpose is to determine whether the changes that occurred in the manufacturing sector increased this sector's pressure on the overall external trade balance. Second, the relationship between manufacturing exports plus non-traditional non-

TABLE 2.18 Manufacturing Imports and Exports: 1971-1981 (millions of dollars)

Year	Exports	Imports	Trade Balance(a)	Trade Balance(b)
1971	119.6	975.7	-856.1	-834.5
1972	82.4	1,125.5	-1,070.1	-1,054.6
1973	84.4	1,356.0	-1,271.1	-1,236.6
1974	290.6	2.050.7	-1,760.1	-1,720.4
1975	390.6	1,084.8	-694.2	-634.0
1976	520.1	1,519.4	-999.3	-919.1
1977	627.6	2,243.7	-1,616,1	-1,516.4
1978	782.0	2,699.0	-1,917.0	-1,763.7
1979	1,245.0	3,904.8	-2,659.8	-2,453.9
1980	1,558.9	4,782.3	-3,223.4	-2,942.5
1981	1,279.6	5,995.8	-4,716.2	-4,389.6

Source: Cortazar, Foxley and Tokman, "Legados del Monetarismo Argentina y Chile," Buenos Aires: Ediciones Solar, 1984, p. 115.

Notes: (a) Includes only manufacturing goods.
(b) Includes non-traditional agricultural exports like fresh fruit, beans, fish, wool and seaweed.

manufacturing exports and manufacturing imports is analyzed. This is because the resource reallocation process did not necessarily have to take place only within the manufacturing sector; resources could be moved into the production of all exportables, from whichever economic sector. The objective here is to take into account the increase in all non-traditional exports and check whether it compensates for the increase in industrial imports.

The results are presented in Table 2.18. They show an increasing deficit between imports and exports of manufacturing goods between 1974 and 1981. After 1978 this deficit was more than three times greater than at the beginning of the 1970s.

It can be argued that the industrial sector's negative impact on the overall balance of payments could have been compensated for by an increase in those non-manufacturing export goods where the country has comparative advantages (fruit, beans, fish, seaweed, etc.). However, as shown in Table 2.18, this does not seem to be the case. The increase of non-manufacturing non-traditional exports was not enough to compensate for the increasing disequilibrium that was being generated in the international trade balance of industrial products.

Hence, our main conclusion is that during the neoconservative experiment the decline in industrial production and employment were not compensated for by increased ability in the non-traditional export sector to generate foreign exchange. It should be noted, however, that in spite of the above conclusion, non-traditional exports did experience a significant increase during the first years of the monetarist experiment. Their share in total output increased by four percentage points between 1970 and 1980 and total exports reached 20 percent of GDP in 1980.

Nonetheless, after 1980 this expansion came to a halt and the diversification achieved in the past showed a tendency to decline. In fact, after 1980 the expansion of exports was mainly based on the production of natural resource intensive goods. As mentioned in several studies,[31] the increase in industrial exports was mainly concentrated in three groups: wood, paper, and food, and only five products accounted for 60 percent of total manufacturing exports.[32]

As analyzed later in Chapter 3, the performance of exports during the neoconservative experiment, briefly described above, is probably the main evidence of the implicit contradictions embodied in the monetarist model. Implementation of the model that claimed to transform exports into the leading growth sector of the economy actually severely lowered the internal relative price of exportables. Potential export firms were thus discouraged from investing in new plants and equipment to become more competitive.

Changes in Productivity and Investments

A third criterion to assess the relationship between the performance of manufacturing and changes in efficiency during 1974–1982 is presented in this section. In particular, I analyze whether the severe decline in industrial jobs was due to adjustments in productive capacity as a result of the opening-up process. According to this argument, external competition forced industrial firms to increase their level of competitiveness by streamlining their production processes and reducing the work force, thus increasing labor productivity.

These arguments will be approached from two points of view. The first is by looking at the performance of investment over time. If firms had to renovate their equipment to adjust to the new conditions, then investment should have increased during this period. The second is by looking at labor productivity figures. The objective here is to analyze whether the deterioration of the manufacturing sector led to increases in productivity above those observed in the past.

Unfortunately, reliable investment data disaggregated by economic activities and aggregated figures for depreciation of the capital stock are not available. Thus, net fixed capital formation cannot be measured. In spite of these problems the performance of investment during the monetarist experiment can be analyzed by looking at the share of gross

TABLE 2.19 Share of Gross Fixed Capital Formation and the Current Account Deficit of the Balance of Payments in GDP

Year	Capital Formation	Current Account Deficit
1960	20.7	4.6
1965	19.9	1.3
1970	20.4	1.5
1973	14.7	3.6
1974	17.4	0.5
1975	15.4	5.6
1976	12.7	-1.9
1977	13.3	3.7
1978	14.5	4.8
1979	15.6	5.9
1980	17.6	8.5
1981	19.5	16.5
1982	15.0	9.5
1960-1970	20.2	2.9
1974-1982	15.7	5.4

Source: Banco Central de Chile, "Cuentas Nacionales de Chile: 1960-1983," Departamento de Publicaciones, Santiago, 1984.

fixed capital formation in GDP. The figures are presented in Table 2.19. They clearly show a sharp decrease in the rate of investment during the monetarist experiment. During the decade of the 1960s the investment coefficient was on average 20.2 percent. This same rate decreased to 15.7 percent between 1974 and 1982. In each of the years of the 1974–1982 period the gross investment rate was below that registered during any year of the 1960s, and in 1981 was still less than in 1970. Moreover, if we take into account the depreciation of machinery and equipment, the situation seems even worse. It has been estimated that the rate of net fixed capital formation decreased from 9.6 percent to 2.9 percent between the decades of the 1960s and the 1970s, respectively.[33] As mentioned above, there are no investment figures available for the industrial sector; however, PREALC (1984) estimates show that the share of new investments in gross manufacturing output decreased from an average of 4.0 percent to 2.76 percent between the periods 1968–1970 and 1977–1979, respectively.[34]

Table 2.19 shows the share of the current account deficit of the balance of payments in GDP. Here I aim to analyze in what proportion this declining investment rate was financed by domestic or external savings. The figures show that in 1970 nearly 90 percent of capital formation was financed with domestic savings. This source of financing decreased significantly after 1974, down to only 50 percent between 1978 and 1981.

The counterpart of this phenomenon is that external savings increased significantly after 1974, and especially after 1978. However, these resources were not used to increase domestic capital formation; rather, they financed an increasing amount of non-traditional imports leading to an appreciation of the real exchange rate and a surge in the balance of payments current account deficit.

To summarize, domestic investment and savings were relatively low during the 1974–1982 period, and the inflow of external capital was used to finance the increasing imports of consumer goods, further contributing to a deterioration in the export sector. Instead of stimulating the growth process, the rising external debt stimulated the current account deficit of the balance of payments and the reduction of productive investment.

I turn now to analyze the relationship between changes in productive capacity and labor productivity. The issue can be stated in the following terms. In spite of the deterioration of the manufacturing sector, reflected in the indicators analyzed previously in this chapter, it could still be argued that those industrial firms that were able to survive went through a series of adjustments in their production processes. Among other things, this implied more efficient utilization of their existing capacity and an increase in labor productivity. Hence, the question is whether labor productivity increased relative to its historical performance.

This question, however, is difficult to answer because there are no reliable productivity figures for the decade of the 1960s. Moreover, the different estimates are not comparable to the figures for the decade of the 1970s. Thus, only a rough approximation to a comparison of these two decades can be made.

During the 1960s the average annual rate of growth of industrial output and employment was 5.3 and 2.9 percent, respectively.[35] Thus, productivity was increasing at a rate of 2.4 percent per year. According to the SOFOFA employment index and my estimations for 1981 and 1982,[36] manufacturing employment decreased at an average annual rate of 5.5 percent between 1974 and 1982.

However, for output there is a discrepancy between the official figures (Central Bank) and a revision of these figures made by Meller, Livacich and Arrau (1984).[37] According to the former, manufacturing output decreased at an average annual rate of 1.8 percent between 1974 and 1982. However, according to the latter, industrial output fell at an annual rate of 4.0 percent during that period.[38] Hence, according to the Central Bank, productivity increased at an average annual rate of 3.7 percent between 1974 and 1982, but according to Meller, Livacich and Arrau (1984), it only rose 1.1 percent per year. Now, if we included other estimates of the performance of industrial employment during 1974–1982, our productivity estimates would have a broader range of variation. Cortazar, Foxley and Tokman (1984) estimate that productivity increased at an average rate of 1.9 percent a year between 1974 and 1982. Hence, we have a variety of results.

However, for reasons that I will explain in the next chapter, it is reasonable to assume that during the 1974–1982 period, when the economy was opening up to international trade, the value added/gross output ratio decreased. If this is the case, the Meller, Livacich, Arrau (1984) estimates are correct, because their method incorporates this effect, while the constant productivity method used by the Central Bank is based on a constant value added/gross output ratio.

For this reason, I conclude that the rate of growth of manufacturing labor productivity during the monetarist experiment most likely decreased or at best it remained the same as in the 1960s.

Conclusions

Three criteria were used in this section to assess whether the contraction of the manufacturing sector during 1974–1982 should be interpreted as part of an efficient resource reallocation process. With respect to the changes in the structure of employment among economic activities, the reduction in employment in the manufacturing sector did not lead to redeployment to other activities, but only to increases in overall unemployment. Regarding the ability of the manufacturing sector to generate foreign exchange, the results showed that the sector contributed to the severe disequilibrium in the country's external commercial balance. With respect to changes in productive capacity, the rate of investment decreased relative to its historical levels and productivity does not seem to have increased above those figures observed in the past.

Hence, the main conclusion of this section is that the monetarist experiment produced a deindustrialization process characterized by the following:

1. Absolute loss of manufacturing jobs without redeployment to other activities, thus contributing to increased overall unemployment;
2. Reductions in the sector's capacity to generate and save foreign exchange, thus contributing to increasing overall external disequilibrium;

3. Deterioration of the sector's productive capacity, thus reducing its future possibilities to increase employment and output.

Notes

1. "ISIC rev. 2" stands for International Standard Industrial Classification revision 2. See United Nations (1968).

2. Following a consensus among Chilean economists, 1970 is used as a benchmark year. It is considered to be a relatively "normal" year and thus can be used as a good representation of the past performance of the economy.

3. "SOFOFA" stands for "Sociedad de Fomento Fabril." It is a private association of industrial producers that surveys 422 firms. However, most of the firms are large (83 percent with 50 or more workers) and the survey represents approximately 60 percent of industrial production. The SOFOFA index incorporates 1,400 types of products.

4. "INE" stands for "Instituto Nacional de Estadisticas" (National Bureau of Statistics). The INE survey covers 420 firms and is also biased towards large firms (50 or more workers in 83 percent of the cases). It also represents about 60 percent of total industrial production and includes only 205 types of products.

5. It will be shown below that this assumption underestimates the productive capacity of the industrial sector in 1974.

6. To have an idea of how large this production loss was, we can compare it with the Chilean external debt in 1982 which was almost 19 billion dollars.

7. Ffrench-Davis (1980), using a similar approach, estimates this decline to be 5 percent between 1971 and 1974.

8. The practical problems associated with the different measures of capacity output are reviewed in Phan-Thuy (1981).

9. An interesting discussion of the advantages and flaws of this method can be read in Klein and Summers (1966) and in Phillips (1963).

10. I come back to analyze this issue in detail in the beginning of Chapter 3.

11. A better procedure would consider the seasonal changes by goods produced. However, the level of aggregation of the available information allows only an analysis of industrial groups at three-digit ISIC rev. 2.

12. The consequences of the financial opening to international markets are analyzed in Chapter 3. See also Chapter 1 for an analysis of the sequence and intensity of the post-1973 stabilization policies. The evolution of the number of firms that went bankrupt is analyzed later in this chapter.

13. In Chapter 1 we characterize this period, 1978–1981, as one in which the economy was supposed to follow the predictions of the "monetary approach to the balance of payments with fixed exchange," also called "global monetarism."

14. There are at least three reasons which justify the exclusion of this sector. First this group includes copper refining, a strategic sector that has increased

its output systematically over time. Second, is the heavy weight it has in the SOFOFA index, and third, it is a sector basically oriented to external markets.

15. The criterion applied to decide whether productive capacity deteriorated or stagnated was the following: Deteriorated groups: Maximum capacity output during 1982–1983 less than or equal to 80 percent of the maximum capacity output during 1969–1973. Stagnant groups: Maximum capacity output during 1982–1983 greater than 80 percent and less than 110 percent of the maximum capacity output during 1969–1973.

16. See Chapter 3 for an attempt to identify the sources of structural change within different manufacturing groups.

17. All the information used in this part of the research was officially provided by the Fiscalia Nacional de Quiebras (Government Office of Bankruptcies). In fact, most of this information was supplied exclusively for this research and has never been published before. I would like to thank the Chairman of this Office, Mr. Rafael Gomez, Ms. Carmen Undurraga and Ms. Isabel Rodriguez for their very useful help in gathering the data.

18. With respect to industry, the 1975 recession had a very strong impact. National GDP decreased by 12.9 and 14.1 percent in 1975 and 1982 respectively and industrial GDP declined 25.5 percent in 1975 and 21.0 percent in 1982.

19. The classification follows the ISIC rev. 2.

20. Between the two censuses there is a compatibility problem with the wood and cork group. In 1967 all the "mobile" sawmills were included, while in 1979 only the ones that had a permanent location were included. This is why this group alone explains 38.3 percent of the total decline in manufacturing establishments between 1967 and 1982. Note also that the decline in this group is concentrated in small firms. (See Table 2.11 wood and cork group.)

21. Unfortunately, more highly disaggregated information by size for total manufacturing is not available.

22. These results are reinforced by the conclusions of other studies. Cortazar, Foxley and Tokman (1984), based on figures for Santiago disaggregated by size, conclude that between 1967 and 1979 the larger establishments experienced a relatively larger reduction in both the number of establishments and in employment, suggesting that an increase in mergers does not explain the decline in the number of establishments. Moreover, they go on to conclude that especially in those establishments with 100 or more employees, the average size decreased proportionately more, suggesting that the reduction of employment was greater than the number of establishments. In terms of manufacturing groups they conclude that Textiles, Machinery, Wood, and Furniture had the largest decrease in the number of establishments. See also PREALC (1984).

23. The last complete survey corresponds to the year 1982. Thus there is a significant delay in the elaboration and publication of these figures.

24. The surveys are only comparable for the following years: 1967 (IV census), 1979 (V census), 1980 (annual survey), 1981 (annual survey), and 1982 (annual survey). They include manufacturing firms with ten or more employees.

25. This group, however, was defined differently in the 1967 and 1979 censuses. (See footnote number 20.)

26. The level of aggregation for bankrupt firms (two digits) is greater than that for employment and the number of establishments (three digits). However, if we aggregate the latter at a two-digit level, we observe a high correlation with those groups that experienced more bankruptcies.

27. See section "The Evolution of Industrial Productive Capacity: 1969–1983" for the criterion used to define a group with deteriorated productive capacity.

28. Sergio de Castro, "The State of Public Finance," in newspaper *El Mercurio,* July 25, 1981. De Castro was the Minister of finance during 1977–1982. Note the date of this quote (July 1981). By that time, the number of bankruptcies had already doubled the numbers observed in the past and the manufacturing sector was showing clear signs of a downturn.

29. The analysis follows Tokman (1984).

30. The figures were taken from Cortazar, Foxley and Tokman (1984) p. 113.

31. See among others Ffrench-Davis (1979), BID (1983), and PREALC (1984).

32. Fish, flour, molybdenum, pine, and cellulose.

33. See Sanfuentes (1983) p. 8.

34. See PREALC (1984) p. 134.

35. The figures were taken from Banco Central de Chile: "Indicadores Economicos y Sociales: 1960–1982" and "Cuentas Nacionales 1960–1983."

36. See Table 2.1 in this chapter.

37. These authors recalculated the national accounts figures for the years 1974–1981 using the double deflation method, rather than the constant productivity method used by the Central Bank. In the next chapter I analyze these issues in detail.

38. Since Meller, Livacich and Arrau (1984) have no estimates for the year 1982, I used the official figure of a −21.6 percent decline of manufacturing value added between 1981 and 1982.

3

Sources of Structural Change in the Manufacturing Sector

The foundations of the neoconservative model were two central structural policies: (1) the opening to international trade and (2) the liberalization of domestic capital markets and the opening-up to external financial markets. In this chapter I concentrate on the impact these two major structural changes had on the industrial sector.

The chapter is divided into two sections. The first begins with a general description of the policies used to open the economy to international trade. I then present the methodology used to quantify the relative impact of the opening-up process on the manufacturing sector. This method is an extension of the Chenery (1980) model, and allows identification and quantification of the relative contribution to gross output of three effects: changes in domestic demand, changes in exports, and changes in import substitution. Hence, this analysis will give us an idea of whether the sources of structural change in the industrial sector were internal or external factors and for the latter, to distinguish between changes in exports and imports.

In the second section I analyze the impact of the financial liberalization process on manufacturing firms. The focus here is on the financial behavior of bankrupt firms. Based on the balance sheets of a sample of bankrupt firms, I construct financial indicators of their debt, profitability, and liquidity and compare them with those of firms that survived.

Opening Domestic Markets to International Trade

The objective of this section is to analyze the effects of the opening-up process on the structure of manufacturing. In particular, the analysis will focus on those manufacturing groups that were relatively more affected by the deindustrialization process. The aim is to identify the relative importance of the external factors as causes of structural change in the industrial sector.

The section is divided into four parts. The first is a brief review of the main characteristics of the opening-up process. The focus is on the type of policies that were implemented, as well as on the results of these measures. In the second part I present the methodology, and in the third, the results. Because the analysis is at the same disaggregation level as in Chapter 2 (three-digit ISIC rev. 2), a comparison is made between the deindustrialization indicators obtained in that chapter and the sources of manufacturing structural change. Finally, this section includes a statistical appendix which explains the sources and methodology used to construct the statistical series.

Characteristics of the Process: Policies and Results[1]

A central element of the transition from a relatively closed to an open economy was the sudden opening of domestic markets to international trade. The objective was to take advantage of the international economy, promoting efficiency and competition through a growth process based on comparative advantages, specialization, and economies of scale. The neoconservative strategy for the opening-up process had two implicit goals: first, to transform exports into the dynamic sector of the economy and second, to increase efficiency in the manufacturing sector. To achieve these objectives the following policies were implemented.

In international trade, non-tariff restrictions were completely eliminated and tariffs were rapidly reduced from the high pre-1973 levels (94 percent on average) to a uniform level of 10 percent, reached in June 1979, for all types of commodities. Exports were promoted via three mechanisms: an initial increase in the real exchange rate, incentives provided by a public institution called "Pro-Chile," and other incentives such as the rebate to exporters of the 20 percent value-added tax. In addition, in 1976 Chile decided to withdraw from the Andean Pact. This pact, with five other Latin American countries, gave preference to Andean production over that of the rest of the world, and set forth a common policy for foreign investment (the so-called Decision 24). This commercial opening-up process was accompanied by encouragement of foreign investment, reduced restrictions on buying and selling foreign exchange, and the sudden opening-up to international financial markets.

Almost all foreign market operations increased during the neoconservative experiment, particularly non-traditional imports and exports.

The expansion of imports was greater than exports, thus, an increasing commercial deficit was generated, especially after 1978. As a consequence of the combined effects of the commercial deficit and the increasing interest payments on private external debt, the net indebtedness position of the country (current account deficit) also worsened. In contrast, the balance of payments (roughly measured by changes in net reserves) showed an increasing surplus. This was the result of the significant increase in capital inflows between 1977 and 1981. However, after the second semester of 1981, international reserves began to decline.

The central policy implemented during the opening-up process was the rapid reduction of protective tariffs that import substitutes had enjoyed until September 1973. The explicit steps of the liberalization policy changed substantially over time. At the beginning of 1974 it was announced that during the next three years a process of tariff reductions was going to take place. In May 1974 it was announced that by 1977 tariffs were not going to exceed 60 percent. Afterwards, in 1975, it was announced that by the first semester of 1978 tariffs were going to be gradually reduced to between 10 and 35 percent. However, the final stages of this reduction process were speeded up, achieving this range in August 1977. Three months later a program of monthly tariff adjustments was announced, which indicated that by June 1979 tariffs were going to reach a level of 10 percent for almost all commodities.

Overall, this process of tariff reduction led to an increase in those imports which had relatively higher levels of effective protection in the past. In particular, industrial imports increased relatively more than agricultural imports, because the latter had negative rates of effective protection. Among manufacturing imports, those that were relatively more protected, e.g. the production of regular consumer goods, increased more.

At the beginning of 1974 it was also officially announced that the real exchange rate was going to increase as effective protection was being reduced. However, in June 1976 the government began using the exchange rate as a policy to break inflationary expectations and to compensate for the monetary effects of the massive capital inflows.[2] As a result of this policy the disequilibrium in the external sector increased and the production of tradables fell. As analyzed in detail in Chapter 1, the exchange rate was fixed in June 1979. In June 1982 the crisis in the productive and financial sectors reached its climax, forcing the authorities to abandon the fixed exchange rate policy and to implement devaluations of more than 70 percent between June and October 1982.[3]

Relative to the level of economic activity, total imports (in real terms) increased considerably. These "new imports" were mainly concentrated in the category of non-food finished consumer goods. The real value of 13 import items, representing 70 percent of total imports of finished consumer goods, increased twelve-fold between 1970 and 1981.

Non-traditional exports increased and products and markets diversified. Their share in the GDP increased by four percentage points between 1970 and 1980, allowing total exports to reach 20 percent of the GDP in 1980. However, at the end of the period this expansion broke down and the diversification process showed a tendency to reverse itself. In fact, those exports that continued to expand were heavily natural resource intensive.

As stated by Ffrench-Davis (1979), just as the import substitution process had an "easy stage," the promotion of exports also had an easy beginning. It seems that the expansion of non-traditional exports during the first years of the neoconservative experiment occurred during this easy stage. In fact, this expansion was based on taking advantage of abundant natural resources and the existence of idle capacity due to the recession of 1975. Among other things, this situation allowed exports to rise without increasing investment. Other factors explaining the expansion of non-traditional exports were the following: the realistic exchange rate policy that was applied at the beginning of the period; the reductions in real wages; the Andean Pact which up to 1976 represented one-third of the market for "new exports," and incentives provided by the government through an institution called "Pro-Chile."

The trade imbalance increased significantly after 1977. Moreover, total imports increased at a faster rate than non-traditional exports, while the quantum of traditional exports remained stagnant. Additionally, favorable terms of trade during the first years of the model helped increase the value of total exports. However, conditions worsened considerably after 1976 when copper prices (representing 50 percent of total exports) dropped sharply.

Opening to international trade had a relatively greater impact on industrial output. Meller, Livacich and Arrau (1984) recalculated the national account figures using the double-deflation method. They found that for the period 1976–1981, the industrial sector grew at an average annual rate of 4.1 percent, which is 40 percent lower than the 6.9 percent calculated by the official figures. These authors argue that the constant productivity method, which is the one used to calculate the official statistics, overestimates the growth rate of the manufacturing sector. The reason given is the following: the constant productivity method assumes that the total input/gross output ratio remains constant over time. However, in an economy experiencing rapid import liberalization, this is not a realistic assumption. The relatively greater use of imported inputs leads not only to substitution for domestic inputs, but also to the elimination of stages in the different production processes. Consequently, imported inputs substitute for domestic factors of production, leading to an increase in the input/gross output ratio and to a decline in the value-added/gross output ratio. Because the double-deflation method assumes variable value-added/gross output coefficients, it better reflects the changes in industrial value-added, which is the relevant indicator in measuring the performance of manufacturing GDP. I turn now to analyze the impact of the opening-up process on the structure of production in the manufacturing sector.

Methodology

During the neoconservative experiment, the manufacturing sector experienced the simultaneous impact of domestic demand restriction and international trade liberalization. In this section I present a methodology that allows separation of these two effects, and the distinction between changes resulting from increases in exports and in import substitution. This quantitative approach to the sources and causes of structural changes is based on a decomposition of the changes in demand. This approach has been widely used in the development literature.[4]

The objective is to differentiate between the contribution of domestic demand (DD), exports (EX) and substitution of imports (IM) to the growth of industrial output. The following variables are defined:

$GO_{i,t}$ = Gross Output of group i in period t.

$M_{i,t}$ = Imports by group i in period t.

$X_{i,t}$ = Exports by group i in period t.

$DD_{i,t}$ = Domestic Demand for goods produced by group i in period t.

The next step is to disaggregate the changes in gross output in each group among DD, EX and IM. Because there is no information available on the different components of domestic demand by manufacturing groups (consumption, investment and intermediate demand), domestic demand (DD) is defined in the following way:

$$DD_{i,t} = GO_{i,t} + M_{i,t} - X_{i,t} \tag{1}$$

The import coefficient is defined as:

$$m_{i,t} = \frac{M_{i,t}}{DD_{i,t}} \tag{2}$$

From (1):

$$GO_{i,t} = DD_{i,t} + X_{i,t} - M_{i,t} \tag{3}$$

Substituting (2) in (3):

$$GO_{i,t} = (1 - m_{i,t}) \times DD_{i,t} + X_{i,t} \tag{4}$$

The objective is to estimate the changes in GO between two periods, t and t+j. Thus, for period t+j:

$$DD_{i,t+j} = GO_{i,t+j} + M_{i,t+j} - X_{i,t+j} \tag{5}$$

Adding and subtracting ($m_{i,t} \times DD_{i,t+j}$) from the right-hand side of equation (5) we obtain:

$$\begin{aligned} GO_{i,t+j} = {} & DD_{i,t+j} \times (1 - m_{i,t}) + X_{i,t+j} \\ & + m_{i,t} \times DD_{i,t+j} - M_{i,t+j} \end{aligned} \tag{6}$$

Subtracting (4) from (6):

$$\begin{aligned} GO_{i,t+j} - GO_{i,t} = {} & (1 - m_{i,t}) \times (DD_{i,t+j} - DD_{i,t}) + \\ & (X_{i,t+j} - X_{i,t}) + (m_{i,t} - m_{i,t+j}) \\ & \times DD_{i,t+j} \end{aligned} \tag{7}$$

Which is the same as:

$$\begin{aligned} \Delta GO_i = {} & (1 - m_{i,t}) \times \Delta DD_i + \Delta X_i \\ & - \Delta m_i \times DD_{i,t+j} \end{aligned} \tag{8}$$

Where:

$$\Delta m_i = m_{i,t+j} - m_{i,t}$$

Thus, the three components of the changes in GO are the following:

(i) DD effect: $(1 - m_{i,t}) \times \Delta DD_i$

(ii) EX Effect: ΔX_i

(iii) IM effect: $\Delta m_i \times DD_{i,t+j}$

Note the minus sign before the IM effect in equation (8). This implies that if $m_{i,t+j} > m_{i,t}$ then IM > 0 and a desubstitution of imports occurs, reducing GO. On the other hand, if $m_{i,t+j} < m_{i,t}$ then IM < 0 and a substitution of imports occurs, increasing GO.

Also note that in equation (8) an index number problem occurs. The problem involves deciding which m_i should be used, in period t or in t+j. To resolve this problem the results are presented with the weights (m_i) of period t (initial period) and of period t+j (final period). The results of both estimations are then compared to check for robustness.

Analysis of the Results

The methodology was applied to the period 1967–1982. The year 1967 is actually an average of the years 1966, 1967 and 1968.[5] The periods were chosen according to the availability of information. Homogeneous series of imports, exports and tariffs disaggregated at a three-digit level are particularly difficult to find. However, the period 1967–1982 is sufficiently long and enables us to compare these results with the ones obtained in Chapter 2. A complete discussion of the sources of information and of the method used to construct the statistical series is presented in the next section.

The results are presented in Table 3.1 (initial weights) and Table 3.2 (final weights). We observe that there are no significant differences between them. Thus, in what follows, the analysis will be based on the results obtained in Table 3.1 (initial weights).

In columns 1, 2, and 3 of this table, the contribution of domestic demand (DD), exports (EX), and substitution of imports (IM) to gross output is presented. Each effect represents the percentage of total output change explained by that effect. In other words, the change in total output (presented in column 4) was made equal to 100 and each effect was calculated as a percentage of total output change.

For example, for the Food group, 19 percent of total output change (25.7 percent) is explained by the increase in domestic demand, 56.5 percent by exports, and 25 percent by import substitution. In columns 5, 6, and 7 the preponderant or main effect is presented. A main effect is defined as one which is the most responsible for the direction in which output changed. Taking again the example of Food, output in this group increased by 25.7 percent, explained mainly by an increase in exports, the preponderant effect.

A general overview of Table 3.1 shows that overwhelmingly, with very few exceptions, domestic demand was the main source of output changes.[6] However, in order to make a more rigorous analysis, it is helpful to classify the manufacturing groups according to whether they experienced increased or decreased output.

TABLE 3.1 Sources of Manufacturing Structural Change: 1967-1982 (a)

	Domestic Demand (1)	Exports (2)	Import Subst. (3)	Output Change (%) (4)	Preponderant Effect DD (5)	EX (6)	IM (7)
Food	19	56.5	25	25.7		x	
Beverage	109	1.7	-11	25.7	x		
Textiles	-81	-6.6	-12	-38.7	x		
Wearing Apparel	-58	0.2	-42	-36.3	x		x
Leather	-80	2.0	-22	-36.1	x		
Footwear	-58	0.1	-42	-30.1	x		x
Wood and Cork	-174	43.1	31	-33.6	x		
Furniture	-149	-0.5	49	-39.6	x		
Paper	33	61.7	6	101.2		x	
Printing and Pub.	-124	-5.8	30	-32.1	x		
Chemicals	-126	27.8	-2	-21.2	x		
Other Chemicals	65	0.6	34	22.8	x		
Petroleum	243	21.9	-165	33.7	x		
Misc. Petrol. and Coal	-101	0.6	0	-88.0	x		
Rubber	-237	-0.6	138	-21.3	x		
Plastic	0	-10.5	111	55.6			x
Pottery, China, Earthen.	-73	6.0	-33	-78.6	x		
Glass	-77	0.2	-23	-50.7	x		
Other Non-Metal. Min.	-179	-1.5	80	-16.0	x		
Iron & Steel Basics	-15	2.1	113	36.7			x
Fabr. Metal Products	-273	10.3	163	-16.7	x		
Machinery	17,373	2,512.5	-19,986	-0.2			x
Electrical Machinery	63	53.1	-16	6.4	x		
Transport	-104	4.0	0	-70.3	x		
Professional Equipment	333	76.2	-509	-41.3			x
Others	5,240	72.3	-5,213	5.7	x		
Total	-278	117.2	60.5	-5.2	x		

Notes: (a) Weights of Initial Period.

In Table 3.3 the results for those manufacturing groups which exhibited decreased output are presented. Part (A) of this table shows those groups that were simultaneously affected by domestic demand and by the opening-up process. In these groups output decreased due to reductions in domestic demand and to the desubstitution of imports. Both effects were very strong, as evidenced by the fact that these groups were among those which experienced the sharpest decreases in output. The range goes from a low of −30.1 percent (footwear) to a high of −78.6 percent in the case of pottery, china and earthenware. Most of these groups produce regular finished consumer goods (textiles, wearing

TABLE 3.2 Sources of Manufacturing Structural Change: 1967-1982 (a)

	Domestic Demand (1)	Exports (2)	Import Subst. (3)	Output Change (%) (4)	Preponderant Effect DD (5)	EX (6)	IM (7)
Food	20	56.5	24	25.7		x	
Beverage	107	1.7	-8	25.7	x		
Textiles	-75	-6.6	-18	-38.7	x		
Wearing Apparel	-47	0.2	-53	-36.3	x		x
Leather	-71	2.0	-31	-36.1	x		
Footwear	-49	0.1	-51	-30.1	x		x
Wood and Cork	-219	43.1	76	-33.6	x		
Furniture	-220	-0.5	120	-39.6	x		
Paper	35	61.7	4	101.2		x	
Printing and Pub.	-144	-5.8	50	-32.1	x		
Chemicals	-125	27.8	-2	-21.2	x		
Other Chemicals	70	0.6	30	22.8	x		
Petroleum	169	21.9	-91	33.7	x		
Misc. Petrol. & Coal	-105	0.6	4	-88.0	x		
Rubber	-381	-0.6	281	-21.3	x		
Plastic	-1	-10.5	111	55.6			x
Pottery, China, Earthen.	-29	6.0	-77	-78.6			x
Glass	-62	0.2	-38	-50.7	x		
Other Non-Metal. Min.	-211	-1.5	113	-16.0	x		
Iron & Steel Basics	-22	2.1	120	36.7			x
Fabr. Metal Products	-411	10.3	301	-16.7	x		
Machinery	12,775	2,512.5	-15,388	-0.2			x
Electrical Machinery	63	53.1	-16	6.4	x	x	
Transport	-105	4.0	1	-70.3	x		
Professional Equipment	37	76.2	-213	-41.3			x
Others	1,336	72.3	-1,308	5.7	x		
Total	-289	117.7	71.2	-5.2	x		

Notes: (a) Weights of Final Period.

apparel, leather, and footwear) and intermediate goods for construction (glass products and pottery, china and earthenware).

Part (B) of Table 3.3 includes those groups that were basically affected by internal recession. The export and import substitution effects contributed positively to gross output in almost all of these groups. In spite of this fact, the negative effect of domestic demand was sufficiently strong to counteract the positive opening-up effect. Thus, output losses were produced, ranging from −16.0 percent (non-metallic minerals) to −88.0 percent (miscellaneous petroleum and coal). These groups, mainly affected by restrictions in aggregate domestic demand, produce inter-

TABLE 3.3 Sources of Structural Change, 1967-1982: Manufacturing Groups with Lower Output (a)

	DD	EX	IM
(A) Negative Domestic Demand, Negative Opening			
Textiles	-81	-6.6	-12
Wearing Apparel	-58	0.2	-42
Leather	-80	2.0	-22
Footwear	-58	0.1	-42
Pottery, China and Earthenware	-73	6.0	-33
Glass	-77	0.2	-23
(B) Negative Domestic Demand, Positive Opening			
Wood and Cork	-174	43.1	31
Furniture	-149	-0.5	49
Printing and Publishing	-124	-5.8	30
Chemicals	-126	27.8	-2
Misc. of Petroleum and Coal	-101	0.6	0
Rubber	-237	-0.6	138
Other Non-Metallic Minerals	-179	-1.5	80
Fabricated Metal Products	-273	10.3	163
Transport	-104	4.0	0
(C) Positive Domestic Demand, Negative Opening			
Machinery	17,375	2,512.5	-19,986
Professional Equipment	333	76.2	-509

Source: Table 3.1.
Note: (a) Initial Weights.

mediate goods for construction (wood and cork, furniture, non-metallic minerals, and metal products), intermediate goods for manufacturing (chemicals and miscellaneous petroleum and coal), and various industrial products like printing and publishing materials, rubber, and transportation equipment. An important exception that stands out from the general pattern described above is the case of wood and cork, where exports played a major role in avoiding a further drop in output.

Finally, Part (C) of Table 3.3 shows those groups that were mainly affected by the opening-up process. In spite of the fact that domestic demand increased, output fell due to a strong process of desubstitution of imports. These groups produce durable consumer goods (machinery) and professional and scientific equipment.

Table 3.4 presents the successful cases, i.e. those groups in which output increased between 1967 and 1982. Part (A) of this table lists four groups in which both domestic demand and the opening-up process

TABLE 3.4 Sources of Structural Change, 1967-1982: Manufacturing Groups with Greater Output (a)

	DD	EX	IM
(A) Positive Domestic Demand, Positive Opening			
Food	19	56.5	25
Paper	33	61.7	6
Other Chemicals	65	0.6	34
Electrical Machinery	63	53.1	-16
(B) Positive Domestic Demand, Negative Opening			
Petroleum	243	21.9	-165
Beverage	109	1.7	-11
Others	5,240	72.3	-5,213
(C) Negative Domestic Demand, Positive Opening			
Iron and Steel Basics	-15	2.1	113

Source: Table 3.1.
Notes: (a) Initial Weights.

contributed to increased output. Two of these groups responded successfully by primarily increasing exports (food and paper). In the case of chemicals, domestic demand was the main source of its output growth, while in the case of electrical machinery, its increase in output was due to a combination of both effects. Part (B) of Table 3.4 lists cases where the process of desubstitution of imports was more than compensated for by the positive effect of domestic demand, thus leading to an increase in output. Finally Part (C) shows the only case (iron and steel basics) where the positive effect of the substitution of imports was strong enough to compensate for the negative effect of domestic recession.

Table 3.5 shows how affected by the period considered these results are. In the first column of this table the results obtained for the 1967–1982 period, analyzed above, are presented. In the second column the results obtained for the 1967–1980 period are presented. (See Table 3.9 in the next section for complete results.) We observe that out of 26 manufacturing groups, only three are classified differently during these two periods (Miscellaneous Petroleum and Coal, Other Non-Metallic Minerals, and Iron and Steel Basics). The rest fall in the same categories. This is a very important conclusion, considering the severe recession that occurred in 1982. On the other hand, the period 1967–1980 (1980 being an average of 1979, 1980 and 1981) encompasses the changes that

TABLE 3.5 Stability of the Results

1967-1982 (a)	1967-1980 (b)
(A) Negative Domestic Demand, Negative Opening	
Textiles	Textiles
Wearing Apparel	Wearing Apparel
Leather	Leather
Footwear	Footwear
Pottery, China and Earthenware	Pottery, China and Earthenware
Glass	Glass
	Misc. of Petroleum and Coal
(B) Positive Domestic Demand, Positive Opening	
Food	Food
Paper	Paper
Other Chemicals	Other Chemicals
Electrical Machinery	Electrical Machinery
Plastic	Plastic
	Other Non-Metallic Minerals
	Iron and Steel Basics
(C) Negative Domestic Demand, Positive Opening	
Wood and Cork	Wood and Cork
Furniture	Furniture
Printing and Publishing	Printing and Publishing
Chemicals	Chemicals
Rubber	Rubber
Fabricated Metal Products	Fabricated Metal Products
Transport	Transport
Misc. of Petroleum & Coal	
Other Non-Metallic Minerals	
Iron and Steel Basics	
(D) Positive Domestic Demand, Negative Opening	
Beverage	Beverage
Petroleum	Petroleum
Machinery	Machinery
Professional Equipment	Professional Equipment
Others	Others

Source: Table 3.1 and Table 3.9.
Notes: (a) 1967 is an average of 1966, 1967 and 1968.
(b) 1980 is an average of 1979, 1980 and 1981.

TABLE 3.6 The Impact of External and Domestic Factors on those Manufacturing Groups Affected by Deindustrialization

	DD	EX	IM	Output Change (%)
Textiles	-81	-6.6	-12	-38.7
Wearing Apparel	-58	0.2	-42	-36.3
Leather	-80	2.0	-22	-36.1
Footwear	-58	0.1	-42	-30.1
Metal Products	-273	10.3	163	-16.7
Machinery	17,373	2,512.5	-19,986	-0.2
Transport Equip.	-104	4.0	0	-70.3
Scientific Equip.	333	76.2	-509	-41.3

Sources: Derived from Table 2.16 and Table 3.1.

occurred between a relatively normal pre-1973 period (average of 1966, 1967 and 1968) and the best years of the neoconservative experiment (1979, 1980 and 1981). In spite of the different characteristics of these periods, the results are remarkably stable. An important element in the stability of the results is the quality of the figures. As mentioned in the next section where the statistical appendix is presented, this is the first time this methodology has been applied with homogeneous figures for imports, exports, tariffs, and prices. The data were gathered directly from reliable sources and no estimations were necessary to construct the series.[7]

In what follows I take a closer look at those manufacturing groups where the deindustrialization phenomenon was relatively stronger. Table 3.6 shows those groups that experienced a severe deterioration in the deindustrialization indicators analyzed in Chapter 2. (See the conclusions of the section on "The Extent of the Decline in Chilean Manufacturing" and especially Table 2.16.)

We observe that out of these eight groups, four of them were affected by restrictions in domestic demand and by a process of desubstitution of imports. These are groups producing regular finished consumer goods like textiles, wearing apparel, leather, and footwear. In other words, these groups were negatively affected by both the opening to international trade and the domestic recession. There were two groups (metal products and transportation equipment) where the decline in domestic demand was the main source of deterioration. Finally, the deindustrialization of the other groups (machinery and scientific equipment) is mainly explained by a strong desubstitution of imports process. In spite of the positive contribution of domestic demand in these two cases, the reduction of tariffs and other forms of protection led to a significant increase in imports and a fall in output. These are groups typically affected by the opening-up process.

Overall, depending on their characteristics, the relative impact of external and domestic factors varies among those groups most severely affected by the deindustrialization phenomenon. In the majority of cases both domestic demand and the opening-up process contributed to their deterioration. However, in other cases, deindustrialization was mainly the result of the isolated effects of domestic demand or the opening-up to international trade.

The main conclusions of this section can be summarized in the following way. First, in terms of the resource reallocation process pursued during the neoconservative experiment, the results show that, at least within the manufacturing sector and with the exception of those traditional exporting groups, exports were not an important source of output change. The dominant influence that increased output in those sectors was the increase in domestic demand, with the exceptions of food and paper, where the expansion of exports has traditionally been a main source of output growth. In the case of wood, exports played a major role in avoiding a further drop in output. In those groups where output decreased, the dominant effects were domestic demand and desubstitution of imports, the former being more important than the latter.

Second, impact was differentiated among those groups where deindustrialization was relatively stronger. Groups producing regular finished consumer goods (textiles, wearing apparel, leather, and footwear) were affected by restrictions in domestic demand and by a desubstitution of imports process, due to the rapid reduction of tariffs and the complete elimination of non-tariff barriers. Those groups producing transportation equipment and metal products were affected mainly by domestic demand, while the opening-up to international trade was the main source of the deterioration experienced by the machinery and scientific equipment industries.

Statistical Appendix

Table 3.7 shows a summary of the sources of information for each variable in the three periods considered. In what follows a detailed explanation of the method used to construct each series is presented.

1. Imports and Exports

1.1. Period 1966–1968:

TABLE 3.7 Summary of Sources of Information and Organization of the Study

	Periods	Tariffs	Gross Output	Imports & Exports	Prices
I)	1966-1968	Corbo & Pollack(1979)	INE: Census 1967	Corbo & Meller(1981)	INE
II)	1979	Aedo-Lagos (1984)	INE: Census 1979		
	1980	10 percent	SOFOFA: Index	ECLA	INE
	1981	10 percent	SOFOFA: Index		
III)	1982	10 percent	SOFOFA: Index	ECLA	INE

The figures used are the ones published by Corbo and Meller (1981). These figures were in escudos of 1967 (the Chilean currency in 1967). To transform them to pesos of 1979, the following method was used:

For Imports

$$M79 = \left[M67 \left((1+s) + \left(\frac{T67}{100} \right) \right) \left(\frac{IPM79}{IPM67} \right) \right]$$

where

M79	=	Imports in thousands of pesos of 1979.
M67	=	Average of imports during the period 1967–1968 in escudos of 1967.
s	=	Freight and insurance equal to a constant 15 percent for all manufacturing groups.
T67	=	Average tariff of the year 1967.
IPM79	=	Wholesale manufacturing price index for the year 1979.
IPM67	=	Wholesale manufacturing price index for the year 1967.

For Exports

$$X79 = X67 \left(\frac{IPM79}{IPM67} \right)$$

where

X79 = Exports in thousands of pesos of 1979.

X67 = Average of exports for the period 1967–1968 in escudos of 1967.

1.2. Period 1979–1981:

Figures provided by the Statistical Division of the Economic Commission for Latin America (ECLA).

This information is classified according to CUCI rev. 2, so it was necessary to transform it to ISIC rev. 2.

Also, the original figures were in dollars of each year. To transform them to pesos of 1979 the following method was used

$$M79_i = (M_i \times tc_i) \quad \left((1 + s) + \left(\frac{T_i}{100}\right)\right) \left(\frac{IPM79}{IPM_i}\right)$$

where

$M79_i$	=	Imports of year i in pesos of 1979.
M_i	=	Imports in dollars of year i.
tc_i	=	Average exchange rate of year i.
T_i	=	Average tariff of year i.
IPM_i	=	Wholesale manufacturing price index of year i.

Then, the average for the period was calculated as

$$M7981 = \frac{1}{3} \sum_i M79_i \qquad i = 1979,\ 1980,\ 1981$$

To adjust the export figures the following method was used:

$$X79_i = (X_i \times tc_i) \left(\frac{IPM79}{IPM_i}\right)$$

where

$X79_i$	=	Exports of year i in pesos of 1979.
X_i	=	Exports in dollars of year i.

Then, the average for the period was calculated.

$$X7981 = \frac{1}{3} \sum_i X79_i \qquad i = 1979,\ 1980,\ 1981$$

1.3. Year 1982:

Same adjustments as period 1979–1981.

2. Tariffs

2.1. Period 1966–1968:

The figures used were obtained from an unpublished study by Corbo and Pollack (1979). The data include the special rights of 1967. This study was made at a four-digit level ISIC rev. 2. To aggregate the information to a three-digit level, the structure of gross output obtained from the IV Manufacturing Census of 1967 (establishments with five or more employees) was used.

Formally:

Define $w_i = \dfrac{GO_i}{GO_j}$

where

w_i	=	Share of gross output of manufacturing group i at four-digit in gross output of group j at three-digit.
GO_i	=	Gross output of group i at four-digit.
GO_j	=	Gross output of group j at three-digit.

Define T_i as the tariff of group i at four-digit.
Thus, the average tariff of group j at three-digit is

$$T_j = \sum_i T_i w_i$$

This is the same method used by Aedo and Lagos (1984) and thus the results are comparable.

2.2. Period 1979–1981:

For the year 1979 the source of information was Aedo and Lagos (1984). The following adjustments were made. First, the classification used by Aedo and Lagos (1984) was made compatible with ISIC rev. 2. (See Table 3.8.) Second, these authors aggregate some groups at the three-digit level. (See Table 3.8.) With tariff information disaggregated at four digits for 1979 and using the method described above, a tariff structure at the three-digit level was constructed for 1979. This structure was used to disaggregate those groups that Aedo and Lagos (1984) had aggregated.

TABLE 3.8 Compatibility of Aedo and Lagos (1984) with ISIC rev. 2

ISIC rev. 2	Aedo and Lago (1984)
Food	Food
Beverage	Beverage
Tobacco	Tobacco
Textiles	Textiles
Wearing Apparel	Wearing Apparel; Footwear
Footwear	
Leather	Leather
Wood and Cork	Wood and Cork
Furniture	Furniture
Paper	Paper
Printing and Publishing	Printing and Publishing
Chemicals	Chemicals; Others Chemicals and Plastic
Others Chemicals	
Plastic	
Petroleum	Petroleum; Misc. of Petroleum and Coal
Misc. of Petroleum and Coal	
Rubber	Rubber
Pottery, China and Earthenware	Pottery, China and Earthenware; Glass; Other Non-Metallic Minerals
Glass	
Other Non-Metallic Minerals	
Iron & Steel Basics	Iron & Steel Basics; Non-Ferrous Metal Industries
Non-Ferrous Metal Industries	
Fabricated Metal Products	Fabricated Metal Products
Machinery	Machinery; Electrical Machinery
Electrical Machinery	
Transport	No information
Professional Equipment	No information
Others	No information

The weights for 1979 were constructed using the V Manufacturing Census (establishments with 10 or more employees).

For the years 1980 and 1981 a tariff of 10 percent was used.

2.3. Year 1982:

Tariffs equal to 10 percent.

2.4. Other Issues:

The tariffs of the groups Transport Equipment, Scientific Equipment, and Others were estimated by using the average annual rate of growth of tariffs for the groups Metal Products, Machinery, and Electrical Machinery.

3. Gross Output

3.1. Period 1966–1968:

It was assumed that the average of the period was equal to 1967 gross output, obtained from the IV National Manufacturing Census (10 or more employees).

To transform these figures to pesos of 1979 the following method was used:

$$GO79 = GO67\left(\frac{IPM79}{IPM67}\right)$$

where

GO79 = Gross output of 1967 valued in pesos of 1979.

GO67 = Value of gross output of 1967.

3.2. Period 1979–1981:

For 1979 the figures were taken from the V National Manufacturing Census of 1979. To calculate the figures for 1980 and 1981, the SOFOFA index of physical production (1969=100) was used. Finally a simple average of the period was calculated for each manufacturing group.

3.3. Year 1982:

Same method as in period 1979–1981.

4. Prices

The average annual prices according to the Wholesale Manufacturing Price Index calculated by INE were used. These indexes are not published and they are calculated by INE to be used exclusively in the elaboration of the national accounts.

5. Other Adjustments

The Tobacco manufacturing group was not included because SOFOFA does not calculate a separate index for this group.

The Plastic manufacturing group was not included because figures for imports and exports were not available.

The manufacturing group Non-Ferrous Metal Industries was not included because the sources used (see Table 3.7) have different definitions for this group, which makes the figures non-comparable.[8]

TABLE 3.9 Sources of Manufacturing Structural Change: 1967-1980 (a)

	Domestic Demand	Exports	Import Subst.	Output Change (%)	Preponderant Effect DD	EX	IM
Food	50.7	36.7	12.5	31.5	x		
Beverage	103.3	5.3	-8.6	50.6	x		
Textiles	-53.3	-8.2	-38.5	-25.7	x		
Wearing Apparel	-53.4	0.9	-47.6	-18.0	x		x
Leather	-46.3	8.3	-62.0	-20.0	x		x
Footwear	-6.0	1.6	-95.6	-6.6			x
Wood and Cork	-261.8	199.6	42.2	-22.7	x		
Furniture	-1,978.2	8.2	1,869.9	-2.0	x		
Paper	34.8	62.7	2.5	131.0		x	
Printing and Pub.	-131.2	-8.4	39.5	-26.3	x		
Chemicals	-17.3	302.8	-185.4	7.0		x	
Other Chemicals	67.1	0.2	32.8	31.0	x		
Petroleum	202.4	7.1	-109.6	81.8	x		
Misc. Petrol. and Coal	-81.3	0.8	-19.5	-85.5	x		
Rubber	-77.9	0.4	177.5	27.2			x
Plastic	22.5	-6.5	84.1	89.2			x
Pottery, China, Earthen.	-69.6	4.8	-35.2	-35.9	x		
Glass	-65.4	8.3	-42.9	-16.6	x		
Other Non-Metal. Min.	49.4	3.8	46.8	38.2	x		x
Iron & Steel Basics	23.3	-5.0	81.7	56.7			x
Fabr. Metal Products	-156.5	29.8	226.7	18.6			x
Machinery	249.9	16.3	-166.2	38.1	x		
Electrical Machinery	75.2	1.9	22.9	116.5	x		
Transport	-104.2	9.2	-5.0	-50.8	x		
Professional Equipment	722.7	59.0	-881.6	-16.5			x
Others	1,478.5	11.7	-1,390.2	19.4	x		
Total	55.9	44.6	-0.5	16.1	x		

Notes: (a) Weights of Initial Period.

Financial Reform: Domestic Liberalization and Opening to International Markets

According to the neoconservatives, one of the main characteristics of the Chilean economy was the existence of "financial repression." They thought that the financial market is a fundamental mechanism in allocating resources, and thus, it should function freely according to supply and demand and not by discretionary state measures. This is why the domestic financial liberalization and the opening-up to external capital markets were major structural reforms implemented during the neoconservative experiment.

The objective of this section is to analyze the effects of these reforms on the manufacturing sector. In particular, we are interested in determining to what extent the financial conditions which prevailed during 1974–1982 altered the behavior of industrial firms, in particular regarding their investment decisions.

The section begins with a description of the main characteristics of the financial reform and the effects it had on the functioning of the capital market. We then focus on the financial behavior of bankrupt firms at a more microeconomic level, comparing financial indicators of bankrupt firms with those of firms that survived. Specifically, we look at the balance sheets of a sample of firms that went bankrupt and calculate liquidity, profitability, and debt indicators and compare them with those of the surviving firms. The section ends with the presentation of the main conclusions.

Characteristics of the Financial Reform

The main criticism of financially repressed markets is based on the effects negative real interest rates have on resource allocation (McKinnon, 1977). According to this view, low or negative real interest rates affect the economy in the following way: They reduce the rate of domestic savings, discouraging the private sector from sacrificing present for future consumption, thus forcing the government to make a greater saving effort. They reduce financial intermediation, leading to the development of capital market segmentation among those who have access to artificially cheap credit and those who have no access at all. Resource allocation thus becomes more inefficient. They reduce the volume of total financial assets in the economy, as measured by indicators like the share of M2 in GDP, which historically has been much lower in Chile than in other developing countries like Taiwan or South Korea. Finally, they cause a low diversification of financial instruments, especially for medium and long-term loans.

Many economists agreed that the Chilean capital market had many deficiencies. However, only the neoconservatives believed that the solution to these problems was to free the functioning of the financial market, leaving it completely in the hands of the market (CEPAL, 1984).

In regards to the degree of control over international capital flows, the financially repressed view is consistent with the argument that in order to take advantage of foreign savings and thus increase the rate of domestic accumulation, capital markets should be open to international financial markets. Thus, controls over these flows should be reduced to minimum levels.[9]

Based on these ideas, financial liberalization and the opening-up to international capital markets began in Chile in 1975, when the first measures were implemented.[10] Most of the banks government-owned during the previous regime were returned or sold to the private sector; interest rates were totally freed; regulations on the terms and allocation of credit were eliminated; new financial institutions were authorized to enter the market with very few limitations; the entrance of foreign banks was encouraged and restrictions on international capital inflows were gradually lifted. Also, the conditions and types of financial operations authorized were gradually made equal for all the institutions, while quantitative controls on credits in domestic currency and on bank reserves were abolished.

With the elimination of previous subsidies and with no discrimination among borrowers, the domestic liberalization of the capital market, accompanied by a gradual opening to external financial markets, was supposed to increase savings together with the quantity and quality of investment.

The results were actually quite different, however. A central aspect of the functioning of the Chilean financial market during the neoconservative experiment was related to the maturity of loans and the interest rates that prevailed. The most frequent term for deposits and loans was of 30 days and the amount of long-term financial intermediation decreased significantly. The real average annual interest rate was around 40 percent during 1975–1981, and fluctuated within a range of 12 to 120 percent.

In other words, domestic real interest rates were extraordinarily high, experiencing great fluctuations over the period. Additionally, the margin of financial intermediation, the difference between the lending (active) and the borrowing (passive) rate, was greater than an annual average of 15 points, which is about three times larger than the normal margin in other countries.

The availability of long-term credit at international interest rates was basically associated with external loans. However, mainly those firms connected with commercial banks and/or with economic groups had access to these loans.[11] This fact gave rise to another kind of market segmentation, this time between those banks and firms who belonged to economic groups and had access to external credit and those who only had access to the domestic market and thus had to pay high interest rates.[12]

One of the objectives of the liberalization and opening-up to international financial markets was to make domestic interest rates equal to international rates. Thus, it was expected that there would be a complete integration of the internal with the foreign market, which would stimulate investment and efficiency. Again, things turned out very differently. The differences between internal and external rates were on average greater than 25 points a year. The domestic market margin of financial intermediation between active and passive rates was around 15 points. Nominal and real rates were very unstable. The volume of credits to buy imported regular and durable consumer goods exhibited the largest increase. The instability and the high cost of credit, together with the fact that most financial operations were of a short-run nature (30 days), discouraged productive investment. What kind of non-financial investment projects could pay average real interest rates above 40 percent per year?[13] As mentioned before, in the section "Productivity and Investments" of Chapter 2 the result was a substantial decrease in the rate of investment during the neoconservative experiment.

Manufacturing Bankruptcies and Financial Behavior[14]

On a general level, the objective of this section is to analyze the impact that the financial reforms had on manufacturing firms. Specifically, the relationship between financial variables and the behavior of bankrupt firms will be analyzed. The objective is to determine the importance of financial factors in explaining the increase in manufacturing bankruptcies during the neoconservative period.

With this purpose in mind, I first analyze the financial performance of firms during the years previous to their bankruptcy. Second, I attempt to identify if there were differences in the financial behavior of firms, according to the years in which their bankruptcies occurred. Finally, I study the impact of the financial reforms on the industrial structure, analyzing the financial behavior among manufacturing groups disaggregated at a two-digit level, ISIC rev. 2.

The method chosen analyzes the balance sheets of a sample of 43 manufacturing firms that went bankrupt during the years 1980, 1981 and 1982. The classification of the sample at a three-digit level and by year of bankruptcy is presented in Table 3.10. For each year I constructed financial indicators of the liquidity, profitability and indebtedness of these firms. I then compare these results with those of a sample of firms that survived.[15]

The results for all the sample are presented in Table 3.11. There we observed that liquidity, as measured by the "acid test" (current assets minus inventory/current liabilities), was extraordinarily low for all manufacturing firms (bankrupt or not). This liquidity test measures the capacity of firms to pay off short-term obligations; thus, the values

TABLE 3.10 Sample of Manufacturing Bankrupt Firms Classified According to ISIC rev. 2. (a)

Groups	Bankrupt in 1980	Bankrupt in 1981	Bankrupt in 1982
Food		- Cia. Arrocera Ega (80) - Arrocera San Fernando	- ULA - Molino Talca - Central Leche Delicias (80)
Textiles	- Cfa. Tex. y Agrfc. - Guanaco - Industria Massu (79) - Emp. Fib. Plast. Tome - Tejidos Viking's	- Sedylan (80)	- Hilanderfa y Tejidos - Safico (80) - Textiles Tala
Wearing Apparel	- Confecciones Casmark	- Soc. Tej. y Vestuarios - Establec. Gaston Rudoff (79-80) - Confecciones Bentex	- Confecciones Oxford - Confecciones Deza
Leather	- Curt. Salavador Caussade		
Footwear	- Calzados Pombo (b)		- Joya (80) - Orlando
Paper			- Papelera Pons
Printing and Publishing		- Soc. A. Grafficas Offset (79-80)	

Industrial Chemicals		- Fab. Nac. Oxfgeno	
Other Chemicals		- Pint. El Adarga (80)	- Ind. Cosmeticos
Rubber		- Ind. Recauch. Conti Rec (79-80)	- Firestone
Plastic			- Implatex - Soc. Revest. Plasticos (79-80) - Man. Plast. Elast. - Calzados Duramil (77)
Glass	- Cristal Yungay		
Fabricated Metal Products	- Fundicion de aceros y metal Fulmet (79)	- Minoxa	- Inmetal - Maestranza Maipu - Metal. Federici (80)
Machinery		- Famatex (80)	- Ind. Artef. Termomec C.
Electrical Machinery			- FRIGICHILE - Ind. Elect. Caro Azar (80)

Source: Data bank from the World Bank project on Liberalization and Stabilization Policies in the Southern Cone.

Notes: (a) The numbers in parentheses represent years for which there are no balance sheets.
(b) Went bankrupt in 1979.

TABLE 3.11 Financial Indicators from a Sample of 43 Bankrupt Manufacturing Firms

Financial Indicators	Bankrupt in 1980			Bankrupt in 1981				Bankrupt in 1982				Surviving Firms	
	1977	1978	1979	1977	1978	1979	1980	1977	1978	1979	1980	1978	1979
1. Liquidity													
Acid Test	0.63	0.79	0.68	0.77	0.54	0.69	0.58	0.51	0.54	0.52	0.68	0.77	0.74
2. Profitability													
Profits/Total Sales	-0.06	-0.06	-0.13	-0.06	0.0	0.02	-0.19	-0.07	-0.04	-0.06	-0.03	0.06	0.05
Profits/Total Equity	-0.28	-0.18	1.80(a)	-0.14	-0.01	0.03	-0.95(b)	-0.10	-0.08	-0.16	-0.08	0.07	0.08
Operational Net Income/ Total Sales	0.03	0.07	0.07	0.11	0.14	0.12	0.02	0.03	0.04	0.05	0.08	-	-
Non-Operational Net Income/Total Sales	-0.11	-0.13	-0.19	-0.17	-0.14	-0.07	-0.22	-0.11	-0.07	-0.10	-0.10	-	-
Financial Expenditures/ Total Sales	0.05	0.19	0.22	0.14	0.14	0.28	0.28	0.05	0.08	0.11	0.13	-	-
3. Indebtedness													
Total Debt/Total Equity	5.76	4.43	-21.46(c)	2.46	3.76	1.81	7.11(d)	1.31	1.82	2.44	1.97	0.56	0.82
Total Debt/Total Sales	1.35	1.51	1.54	1.01	0.97	1.28	1.45	0.88	0.81	0.89	0.85	0.46	0.84
Bank Debt/Total Debt	0.42	0.44	0.60	0.36	0.42	0.47	0.42	0.45	0.54	0.55	0.52	-	-

Sources: The raw data for bankrupt firms (1980, 1981 and 1982) was provided by the Data Bank of the World Bank project on Liberalization and Stabilization Policies in the Soutern Cone. The indicators were constructed by the author.

Surviving firms in 1978: SOFOFA, Special Survey Number 4, August, 1979. Includes those firms which had profits (81.5 percent of the sample) and those with losses (18.5 percent of the sample).

Surviving firms in 1979: SOFOFA, Special Survey Number 5, July, 1980. Includes only those firms which had profits (84.4 percent of sample).

Notes: (a) This value is explained because during this year firms had losses and total equity was negative.

(b) This value is explained because during this year all firms had losses in spite of the fact that total equity was positive and did not change with respect to 1979.

(c) Explained because of a strong increase in total debts between 1978 and 1979 and total equity decreased becoming negative.

(d) Explained because between 1979 and 1980 total equity decreased by 80 percent and total debt by 21.5 percent. Also, seven firms did not have balance sheets for 1980.

shown in row 1 of Table 3.11 indicate that on average industrial firms needed to go into debt to finance their need for working capital and short-term payments. We also observe that the liquidity position of bankrupt firms was worse than for firms which survived; however, it should be noted that the situation of the latter was still quite precarious.

In row 2 of Table 3.11 profitability ratios have been calculated. We observe that both the ratio of profits to total sales and the ratio of profits to total equity were negative. On the other hand, firms that survived had profitability ratios that fluctuated between 5 and 8 percent. In other words, bankrupt firms had lower rates of profit than average manufacturing firms.

However, it is interesting to compare a firm's operating net income with the net income associated with non-operational activities, since financial expenditures are especially important among the latter. In row 2 of Table 3.11 the ratio of operational and non-operational net income to total sales are presented respectively. We observe that the former were all positive, while the latter were all negative. This phenomenon can be explained by the high proportion of financial expenditures in total sales, which in turn was the result of the high degree of indebtedness and the high interest rates which prevailed in the financial markets. (See the ratio of financial expenditures to total sales in row 2 of Table 3.11.)

The third group of financial ratios is associated with the degree of firm indebtedness. (See row 3 of Table 3.11.) Two indicators have been calculated for this purpose. First, the ratio of total debt to firm equity was greater for bankrupt firms than for firms that survived. Second, the ratio of total debt to total sales shows that in general, firms that went bankrupt had a larger share of their sales committed in the form of debts than firms that survived. In addition, approximately half of bankrupt firm debt was with commercial banks. Comparing this last result with the ones obtained by Mizala (1985) for a sample of firms that survived, it is possible to conclude that the degree of indebtedness of these firms to commercial banks was much less than that for bankrupt firms. This is probably a very important factor in explaining the severity of the financial crisis of 1982. The analysis of the composition of firms' debts shows that short-term indebtedness increased in its importance relative to total debt. This fact is substantiated by our previous results showing the lack of liquidity and profitability, which led to short-term credits becoming increasingly the most important source of financing.

The analysis of the financial indicators by year of firm bankruptcy shows that there are no substantial differences among them, suggesting

TABLE 3.12 Composition of Assets: Bankrupt Firms versus Firms Which Survived, 1977-1982

	Assets (a) (1977=100)		Percentages over Total Assets			
	Total (1)	Fixed (2)	Financial Assets (3)	Assets in Related Firms (4)	Total Debt (5)	Inventories (6)
Bankrupt during 1979-1980						
1977	100.0	100.0	0.0	0.0	85.2	27.2
1978	118.5	128.2	0.5	0.4	81.6	22.6
1979	105.9	114.7	0.0	0.0	104.9	25.2
Bankrupt during 1981-1982						
1977	100.0	100.0	1.5	0.3	60.8	20.8
1978	103.7	91.5	0.8	0.5	69.3	21.5
1979	115.6	92.9	10.2	9.9	68.9	21.2
1980	107.1	93.3	7.1	6.5	71.1	19.7
Total Sample of Firms Survived						
1977	100.0	100.0	17.8	9.2	45.3	18.7
1978	95.1	87.4	19.9	9.2	48.2	17.5
1979	111.5	90.9	26.0	18.2	47.7	16.4
1980	125.2	91.4	28.4	20.7	47.7	15.3
1981	117.7	91.5	26.3	23.7	55.7	13.4

Source: Mizala, A. "Liberalizacion Financiera y Quiebra de Empresas Industriales: Chile, 1977-1982. Notas Tecnicas CIEPLAN No. 67, Enero, 1985, Cuadro 3.

Note: (a) Real Values deflated by the Consumer Price Index of Cortazar and Marshall (1980).

that the financial reasons for the bankruptcies of firms in 1982 are basically the same as for the years 1980 and 1981.

From the point of view of the study of Chilean deindustrialization, it is interesting to analyze the implications these results have for variables determining the behavior of the real side of the economy. Because the relevant financial indicators show important differences between firms that went bankrupt and firms that survived, we will attempt to analyze the implications of these differences, in particular, their impact on investment.

Table 3.12 gives the necessary information to assess this issue. We observe that the probability of survival was associated with a recomposition of firm assets, specifically, a substitution away from fixed assets (land, infrastructure, machinery, and equipment) toward financial assets. Those financial assets, given the conditions offered in the financial markets, were much more profitable. Firms that survived decreased their fixed assets in absolute terms, from a level equal to 100 in 1977 to 91.5 in 1981. (See Table 3.12, column 2.)

On the other hand, bankrupt firms did not significantly alter their asset composition. In fact, the ones that went bankrupt in 1979–1980 did exactly the reverse of those that survived, as they increased their fixed assets from a level equal to 100 in 1977 to 114.7 in 1979. (See Table 3.12, column 2.) Moreover, as shown in Table 3.12, column 3, bankrupt firms' share of financial assets in total assets was not only relatively lower in terms of levels, but also increased at a slower rate than that of surviving firms. Finally, in column 6 of the same table, we observe that bankrupt firms' share of inventories in total assets was practically stable while for those firms that survived, this rate decreased from 18.7 percent in 1977 to 13.4 percent in 1981.

To summarize, it seems that one of the mechanisms used by firms to survive was to maintain a high proportion of financial assets, taking advantages of extraordinarily high interest rates and thus postponing productive investment decisions for the future. Paradoxically, relative prices were indicating that the best alternative was not to invest in machinery and equipment, even if this were to increase a firm's competitive position. It seems that rational maximizing financial management dictated an increase in a firm's liquidity so as to allow more funds to be deposited in the capital market, thus taking advantage of the extraordinary short-term capital gains made possible by the high interest rates.[16]

We turn now to analyze the financial behavior of bankrupt firms in certain manufacturing groups. Because of the size of the sample,[17] we will look at four groups disaggregated at a two-digit level ISIC rev. 2: Food, Beverage and Tobacco; Textiles, Wearing Apparel and Leather; Chemicals, Petroleum, Coal, Rubber and Plastic; and Fabricated Metal Products, Machinery and Equipment. The results are presented in Tables 3.13, 3.14, 3.15 and 3.16 respectively.

The first thing to notice is that on a general level, the financial performance of bankrupt firms in these four manufacturing groups was basically very similar to the behavior of manufacturing as a whole. With few exceptions, the financial ratios in each group behaved in the same way as the averages for total industry. This fact suggests that the financial reform had similar effects among different industrial groups, leading us in turn to think that the differences in manufacturing groups' performance is not explained by the financial reform. Rather, it seems

TABLE 3.13 Financial Indicators of Group: Food, Beverage and Tobacco

Financial Indicators	Bankrupt in 1981				Bankrupt in 1982				Surviving Firms	
	1977	1978	1979	1980	1977	1978	1979	1980	1978	1979
1. Liquidity										
Acid Test	0.32	0.68	0.40	0.14	0.62	0.54	0.29	1.08(a)	0.75	0.82
2. Profitability										
Profits/Total Sales	-0.06	0.02	0.01	-0.17	-0.03	-0.03	-0.17	0.02	0.05	0.07
Profits/Total Equity	-0.15	0.07	0.02	-0.67	-0.10	-0.12	-5.17(b)	0.06	0.06	0.12
Operational Net Income/ Total Sales	0.02	0.17	0.13	0.12	-0.03	-0.01	-0.15	-0.06	-	-
Non-Operational Net Income/Total Sales	-0.07	-0.14	-0.11	-0.28	0.0	-0.01	-0.01	0.07	-	-
Financial Expenditures/ Total Sales	0.05	0.09	0.16	0.23	0.01	0.02	0.13	0.09	-	-
3. Indebtedness										
Total Debt/Total Equity	1.09	1.18	1.69	3.25	0.71	1.41	14.71(c)	1.52	0.69	0.81
Total Debt/Total Sales	0.42	0.41	0.55	0.80	0.21	0.31	0.48	0.43	0.50	0.63
Bank Debt/Total Debt	0.39	0.12	0.83	0.34	0.39	0.51	0.48	0.62	-	-

Sources: The raw data was provided by the Data Bank of the World Bank project on Liberalization and Stabilization Policies in the Southern Cone. The indicators were constructed by the author.

Surviving Firms in 1978: SOFOFA, Special Survey Number 4, includes those firms which had profits (81.5 percent of the sample) and those with losses (18.5 percent of the sample).

Surviving Firms in 1979: SOFOFA, Special Survey Number 5, includes only firms with profits (84.4 percent of the sample).

Notes: (a) Explained because one firm did not have a balance sheet for the year 1980. Also current liabilities of "ULA", the most important firm of the sample, experienced a sharp fall between 1979 and 1980 (75.9 percent) and its Current Assets increased significantly between those years (187.1 percent).

(b) Explained by a sharp fall in equity between 1978 and 1979 (78.2 percent) and an increase in losses (811.5 percent). These variations are basically explained by firm "ULA". (See note (a).)

(c) Explained by the same reasons as Note (b). Big jumps associated with the most important firm of the sample, "ULA".

that it was the opening to international trade that had a more varied effect from group to group. As mentioned in the section "The Evolution of Bankruptcies and Number of Establishments" of Chapter 2, manufacturing bankruptcies were concentrated in Textiles, Wearing Apparel and Leather and Fabricated Metal Products, Machinery and Equipment, which, given the types of goods they produce and their characteristics, were especially affected by external competition.[18]

The second point that needs to be emphasized is that the lack of liquidity was a problem that affected all groups in a similar way. For all the groups, the value of the "acid test" are less than zero and less than the ones obtained for those firms that survived. Undoubtedly, the need to finance working capital is a very important reason in explaining the bankruptcies of firms.

With respect to profitability (measured by the ratio of profits to total sales and equity) we observe that in general, all groups had negative ratios, a fact which eliminated the possibility of financing working capital with profits. Moreover, bankrupt firm profits were much less than for the average manufacturing firm. However, considering the severity of this problem, the only group that showed profitability ratios greater than the average was Fabricated Metal Products, Machinery and Equipment, especially those firms that went bankrupt in 1981. This fact probably explains why this group also shows liquidity ratios a little higher than the group's average.

The comparison of operational and non-operational net income, both as a percentage of total sales, shows two types of behavior among groups. First, Food, Beverage and Tobacco (Table 3.13) is characterized by negative operational and non-operational net income ratios, in particular, in those firms which went bankrupt in 1982. Second, in the rest of the groups, we observe the same pattern followed by the average bankrupt manufacturing firm, i.e. positive operational net income ratios and negative non-operational net income ratios. These results suggest that the former were in a worse situation than the latter, because they needed to get into debt not only to cover their non-operational deficits, but also to finance the regular operational activity of the firm. However, this phenomenon was not reflected in greater debt ratios for these firms. The reason for this is that the magnitude of the debt ratio depends on the size of the non-operational deficit relative to operational net income. In fact, those groups with greater debt ratios had positive and negative (greater than the industrial average) operational and non-operational net income ratios respectively. The reason is that the latter were much greater than the former. This phenomenon is substantiated by the fact that these groups had relatively greater shares of financial expenditures in total sales.

TABLE 3.14 Financial Indicators of Textiles, Wearing Apparel and Leather Group

Financial Indicators	Bankrupt in 1980			Bankrupt in 1981				Bankrupt in 1982				Surviving Firms	
	1977	1978	1979	1977	1978	1979	1980	1977	1978	1979	1980	1978	1979
1. Liquidity													
Acid Test	0.64	0.83	0.74	0.88	0.80	0.67	0.60	0.50	0.49	0.56	0.79	0.69	0.74
2. Profitability													
Profits/Total Sales	-0.05	-0.06	-0.09	-0.08	-0.01	0.02	-0.17	-0.17	-0.02	-0.09	-0.23	0.01	0.02
Profits/Total Equity	-0.22	-0.18	12.22(a)	-0.16	-0.0	0.03	-0.67	-0.72	-0.17	-1.17(b)	9.02(c)	0.01	0.03
Operational Net Income/ Total Sales	0.06	0.13	0.09	0.14	0.14	0.16	0.05	0.01	0.08	0.05	0.07	-	-
Non-Operational Net Income/Total Sales	-0.12	-0.19	-0.17	-0.22	-0.15	-0.04	-0.21	-0.18	-0.08	-0.14	-0.30	-	-
Financial Expenditures/ Total Sales	0.11	0.26	0.21	0.18	0.14	0.33	0.24	0.11	0.08	0.13	0.34	-	-
3. Indebtedness													
Total Debt/Total Equity	6.14	4.60	-230.21(d)	2.48	3.85	1.46	5.28	4.60	7.70	14.97(e)	-61.47(f)	0.74	0.84
Total Debt/Total Sales	1.41	1.67	1.69	1.21	1.05	1.36	1.32	1.07	0.99	1.16	1.54	0.46	0.90
Bank Debt/Total Debt.	0.45	0.46	0.63	0.38	0.44	0.43	0.44	0.34	0.36	0.60	0.46	-	-

Sources: The raw data for bankrupt firms (1980, 1981, 1982) was provided by the Data Bank of the World Bank Project on Liberalization and Stabilization Policies in the Southern Cone. The indicators were constructed by the author.

Surviving Firms in 1978: SOFOFA, Special Survey Number 4, includes firms with profits (81.5 percent of the sample) and with losses (18.5 percent of the sample).

Surviving Firms in 1979: SOFOFA, Special Survey Number 5, includes only firms with profits (84.4 percent of the sample).

Notes: (a) Explained by an increase in losses and a sharp drop in equity which becomes negative in 1979.
(b) Explained because losses increased by 477.5 percent between 1978 and 1979.
(c) Losses continue to increase and equity becomes negative.
(d) The performance of "Tome" and "Curtiembre S. Caussade" explain this value. In particular equity becomes negative.
(e) Explained by a strong increase in total debts between 1978 and 1979.
(f) Equity continues to fall becoming negative. Also, the sample is reduced because two firms did not have balance sheets for this year.

TABLE 3.15 Financial Indicators of Chemicals, Petroleum, Coal, Rubber and Plastics Group

Financial Indicators	Bankrupt in 1981				Bankrupt in 1982				Surviving Firms	
	1977	1978	1979	1980	1977	1978	1979	1980	1978	1979
1. Liquidity										
Acid Test	0.54	0.59	0.64	0.23	0.45	0.51	0.48	0.53	0.91	0.42
2. Profitability										
Profits/Total Sales	-0.02	-0.04	-0.03	-0.04	-0.10	-0.03	0.01	-0.02	0.01	0.05
Profits/Total Equity	-0.06	-0.21	-0.18	-0.31	-0.99	-0.04	-0.01	-0.03	0.01	0.11
Operational Net Income/ Total Sales	0.0	0.0	-0.05	-0.26(a)	0.07	0.05	0.11	0.09	-	-
Non-Operational Net Income/Total Sales	-0.01	-0.04	0.02	0.21	-0.17	-0.09	-0.10	-0.10	-	-
Financial Expenditures/ Total Sales	0.01	0.04	0.15	0.41	0.06	0.11	0.05	0.05	-	-
3. Indebtedness										
Total Debt/Total Equity	4.44	6.02	7.85	18.8(a)	1.18	1.30	1.40	1.31	0.69	0.81
Total Debt/Total Sales	1.03	1.08	1.43	2.60	1.30	0.95	0.91	0.81	0.33	1.09
Bank Debt/Total Debt	0.20	0.19	0.05	0.06	0.52	0.67	0.60	0.62	-	-

Sources: The raw data was provided by the Data Bank of the World Bank project on Liberalization and Stabilization Policies in the Southern Cone. The indicators were constructed by the author.

Surviving Firms in 1978: SOFOFA, Special Survey Number 4, includes those firms which had profits (81.5 percent of the sample) and those with losses (18.5 percent of the sample).

Surviving Firms in 1979: SOFOFA, Special Survey Number 5, includes only firms with profits (84.4 percent of the sample).

Note: (a) Two firms did not have balance sheets for this year.

TABLE 3.16 Financial Indicators of Fabricated Metal Products, Machinery and Equipment Group

Financial Indicators	Bankrupt in 1980			Bankrupt in 1981				Bankrupt in 1982				Surviving Firms	
	1977	1978	1979	1977	1978	1979	1980	1977	1978	1979	1980	1978	1979
1. Liquidity													
Acid Test	0.49	0.54	-	0.76	0.90	0.89	0.74	0.68	0.58	0.73	0.78	0.83	0.97
2. Profitability													
Profits/Total Sales	0.07	0.03	-	0.01	0.05	0.04	-0.58	0.02	-0.12	-0.07	-0.01	0.05	0.05
Profits/Total Equity	0.13	0.03	-	0.03	0.33	0.18	2.48(a)	0.03	-0.32	-0.23	-0.03	0.07	0.08
Operational Net Income/ Total Sales	0.31	-0.01	-	0.17	0.22	0.02	-0.09	0.02	0.03	0.13	0.17	-	-
Non-Operational Net Income/Total Sales	-0.24	-0.05	-	-0.17	-0.17	-0.21	-0.48	-0.09	-0.14	-0.21	-0.11	-	-
Financial Expenditures/ Total Sales	0.21	0.03	-	0.16	0.21	0.25	0.58	0.05	0.13	0.22	0.22	-	-
3. Indebtedness													
Total Debt/Total Equity	5.17	1.34	-	4.63	7.68	7.26	-10.39(b)	1.18	2.41	3.07	2.69	0.13	1.92
Total Debt/Total Sales	2.77	1.51	-	0.86	1.08	1.59	2.42	0.76	0.91	0.96	0.82	0.11	0.93
Bank Debt/Total Debt	0.0	0.0	-	0.35	0.54	0.72	0.61	0.85	0.45	0.27	0.17	-	-

Sources: The raw data for bankrupt was provided by the Data Bank of the World Bank project on Liberalization and Stabilization Policies in the Southern Cone. The indicators were constructed by the author.

Surviving Firms in 1978: SOFOFA, Special Survey Number 4, includes those firms which had profits (81.5 percent of the sample) and those with losses (18.5 percent of the sample).

Surviving Firms in 1979: SOFOFA, Special Survey 5, includes only firms with profits.

Notes: (a) Positive results because losses increased and equity became negative.

(b) The sample is reduced by one firm, which makes equity decline by 183.2 percent between 1979 and 1980.

Finally, it is important to notice that the combination of high debt and low liquidity ratios, a greater share of financial expenditures in total sales, and positive and negative operational and non-operational net income ratios is clearly observed in Textiles, Wearing Apparel and Leather and in Fabricated Metal Products, Machinery and Equipment. For these two groups the sample was disaggregated at a three-digit level (ISIC rev. 2), but no substantial differences with the conclusions obtained at a two-digit level were found.

Conclusions

In this section, we have attempted to make the following points. First, it is clear that those firms that went bankrupt had serious liquidity problems. In all the years the "acid test" shows values less than one, which means that these firms were operating with negative net working capital. Second, the profitability of these firms was negative and much less than the average of the manufacturing sector. Negative profits have a double effect. On the one hand, the possibility of using profits as a source of financing additional working capital is eliminated. On the other hand, the possibility of obtaining long-term credit is severely reduced, forcing firms to increase their short-run indebtedness to finance their need for working capital. Third, the high cost of credit generated a short-run indebtedness spiral to pay interest and finance liquidity needs which only ended when firms went bankrupt. This fact is substantiated by our results on the high and increasing share of financial expenditures in total sales. Fourth, the above conclusions suggest that the level of indebtedness was unsustainable, reaching in some cases four and five times the equity of the firms. Fifth, bankrupt firms maintained a relatively greater share of fixed assets than firms which survived. This was possible because of the great availability of credit. However, as analyzed in Chapter 4, the increase in fixed assets financed through indebtedness, especially in dollars, is a very important factor in explaining firm bankruptcies.

One of the adjustment mechanisms used by some firms to increase their level of competitiveness was to renovate their equipment and machinery. With this objective in mind, these firms decided to get into debt denominated in dollars. The measures which regulated access to these loans made it very easy for firms to go into dollar debt. However, because of the over-valued exchange rate and the wage policies in effect since 1978, average firm costs increased at a faster rate than average prices, making the production of exportable goods less profitable. The devaluation of the peso in June 1982 was the last and final call for these firms, as their debts reached levels which made their operations totally unfeasible.

This is how the results of the macroeconomic policy determined a set of relative prices which were in contradiction with the assumption of the neoconservative model. Interest rates did not converge to international rates. Instead, throughout the whole period, domestic rates were extraordinarily high, thus encouraging short-run financial investment and discouraging productive investment. Domestic prices did not converge to international prices. This factor, accompanied by the fixed exchange rate policy, severely deteriorated the profitability and competitiveness of all tradables, including exportables, which according to the assumptions of the model, were to become the leading growth sector in the economy. The adjustment process did not take place according to the predictions of the model, increasing considerably the costs of reallocating resources.

Notes

1. This section is based on Ffrench-Davis (1979), Ffrench-Davis (1980), and CEPAL (1984).

2. The erratic character of the opening-up process raises important questions about the credibility the new policies held for entrepreneurs.

3. A detailed explanation of the functioning of the Chilean economy under a fixed exchange rate system is presented in Chapter 1.

4. This method was initiated by Chenery (1980). For applications of this methodology see Corbo and Pollack (1982) and Vergara (1980).

5. The method was also applied during the time between the averages of the years (1966, 1967 and 1968) and (1979, 1980 and 1981). However, as analyzed below, the results do not change significantly and they will be used mainly to support the results obtained for the 1967–1982 period.

6. Corbo and Pollack (1982) and Vergara (1980) for the period (1969–1970), (1978–1979) found the same results. My results for the period (1966–1968), (1979–1981) show the same thing. (See Table 3.9 in the next section.)

7. This is probably the main difference between this study and other research done on Chile where this methodology was applied. Corbo and Pollack (1982) and Vergara (1980) had to rely on estimates for imports and exports based on the input/output coefficients of the 1977 matrix.

8. The statistical series is available from the author.

9. There was, however, disagreement regarding the order of economic liberalization in different markets. Some thought that the goods market should be opened first and then the financial market progressively opened. Others regarded the financial opening as a key measure to increase investment in the tradable sector; thus, the commercial opening should go second. (See McKinnon, 1982 and CEPAL, 1978.)

10. This part and the figures presented are based on Ffrench-Davis and Arellano (1981).

11. This fact was only publicly recognized by the second semester of 1982 when it was disclosed that the biggest bank of one economic group had 44 percent of its total loans (financed with internal and external funds) in related enterprises, i.e. by the same owners and board of directors.

12. An interesting analysis of the development of the economic groups can be found in Dahse (1979). The relationship between external loans, commercial banks and firms owned by economic groups is studied in Herrera and Morales (1979).

13. The question of the determinants of the persistently high real interest rates during 1974–1982 have spurred an interesting discussion in the literature. See Ffrench-Davis and Arellano, 1981; Sjaasstad and Cortes, 1978; CEPAL, 1984; Zahler, 1980; McKinnon, 1977; and Tapia, 1979.

14. I would like to acknowledge the statistical work of Veronica Letelier in this section.

15. The financial indicators of firms that survived were taken from Espinosa, Gonzalez and Morales (1982) and Special Surveys made by SOFOFA.

16. This issue was repeatedly brought up in the interviews of entrepreneurs of firms which survived. See the case study section of Chapter 4.

17. See Table 3.10 in this section.

18. Note also that the greater importance of these two groups is well reflected in the sample of firms used to analyze the financial behavior of bankrupt firms. (See Table 3.10.)

4

Case Studies

This chapter begins with a look at the bankruptcy procedure in Chile and analyzes the ways in which this process affected those firms that went bankrupt. Because the number of bankruptcies is one of the indicators used to show the magnitude of the deindustrialization phenomenon, it is interesting to have a broader understanding of the special characteristics of the bankruptcy process during the neoconservative experiment. This study in turn will be useful to support the findings of the previous chapters with a more qualitative analysis.

Based on case studies of bankrupt firms, I then analyze their experiences and the type of adjustments made by these firms. The objective is to follow their reactions and adjustments to the new economic conditions, trying to determine the type of changes that occurred in the operations of these firms.

The Bankruptcy Procedure and Its Impact on a Sample of Firms

The objective of this section is to study more deeply the economic meaning of bankruptcies. In particular, an assessment is made of the number of bankrupt firms, as an indicator of deindustrialization. I first analyze the bankruptcy procedure according to Chilean law. I then attempt to identify the implications this procedure had on the functioning of manufacturing firms going bankrupt. I look at the experiences of these firms, trying to determine how their normal functioning was altered by the bankruptcy process.

The information used in this section comes from three separate sources. The bankruptcy laws, interviews with two lawyers and one economist working in the *Fiscalia Nacional de Quiebras* (Government Agency of Bankruptcies), and interviews with previous owners and executives of several bankrupt firms.

The Legal Procedure

The bankruptcy procedure in Chile is ruled by the law of bankruptcies Number 18.176 of October 1982, which replaced law number 4558 from June 23, 1931.[1]

According to the present law, "the objective of a bankruptcy trial is to liquidate, in only one procedure, the assets of a natural or juridical person, to pay for their debt in the cases and ways determined by the law" (Law 18.175, article 1). With respect to the assets involved in the bankruptcy procedure, the law establishes that "the situation of bankruptcy produces an indivisible state for the bankrupt firm and the creditors. Consequently, all the assets and obligations of the former, even the ones without a due term, are part of the bankruptcy process, with the only exceptions established in the law" (Law 18.175, article 2).

The law of bankruptcies was updated because the economic authorities in 1982 thought that the old law was out of step with the changes that had taken place in the functioning of markets and commercial operations. In other words, another law that would respond to the new economic conditions was needed. This is why one of the main objectives of the new law was to "gain speed and efficiency in the implicit process of reallocating resources that is involved in every bankruptcy."[2] Before the law was changed, the average length of time of resolution of a bankruptcy was five years. At the moment the new law was put into effect in February 1983 the 1,500 to 1,600 bankruptcies that were being administered under the old law were transferred to the new one.

It is interesting to note the dates on which both laws were dictated, the first one in June 1931 and the second in October 1982. Both of these periods were characterized by severe recessions and by a considerable increase in the number of bankruptcies, which, among other things, determined the need for legislation. In the first case, the legislation which was going to rule the bankruptcy procedure for the next 51 years was created. In the second case, the new law was created in order to shorten the time of the bankruptcy process. This was necessary because, as we saw in the section "The Evolution of Bankruptcies and Number of Establishments" in Chapter 2, the number of bankrupt firms increased significantly after 1978.

In order to give a general idea of the contents of these laws, I will briefly mention the main modifications made in the old law.

- A new institution called Fiscalia Nacional de Quiebras (Government Agency of Bankruptcies) was created under the Ministry of Justice. This agency's main purpose is to supervise and control the persons appointed as official receivers (*sindicos*), especially in those technical, juridical and financial issues related to bankruptcy administration.

- The requirement that the official receivers had to be public employees was eliminated. Under the new law the official receivers represent both the general interest of the creditors and the rights of the bankrupt parties. Some of the main duties of the official receivers are: to make an inventory of the assets of the bankrupt person or company and to manage them according to the law; to temporarily continue the operations of the bankrupt firm; and to liquidate the goods and commodities involved in the bankruptcy.
- The steps necessary to liquidate the assets of the bankrupt party were greatly simplified.[3]
- The creditors are now required to pay for the initial steps of the bankruptcy process. The objective of this measure was to eliminate the possibility of using the bankrutpcy procedure as a judicial mechanism to recover debts.

Most of the government employees interviewed agreed that in practice the most important difference between the two laws is the fact that the official receiver could now be any person, previously accepted by the Ministry of Justice as qualified and nominated by the court that declares the bankruptcy. The official receiver actually administers the bankruptcy and the Fiscalia basically supervises the actions of the official receivers.[4] Additionally, the creditors are more actively incorporated into the bankruptcy procedure under the new law.

From this brief description of the major changes that occurred in the bankruptcy legislation, it is possible to conclude that the new law reflects the ideas of the economic authorities of that time. The new law reduces the role of the government, transferring some of the main decisions involved in the procedure to the private sector, in this case to the parties involved in a bankruptcy. From the point of view of the results of a bankruptcy, this is a very important point. As analyzed below, the decisions on the ways and conditions in which the machinery and equipment of the bankrupt firm were liquidated were now basically left up to the parties involved in the process.

Classification of Bankrupt Firms

For the purpose of this section, which is to determine to what extent bankruptcies are a relevant indicator in measuring the magnitude and intensity of the deindustrialization process, bankrupt firms can be classified into three types: (1) Firms with Released Bankruptcies, (2) Firms Declared Economic Units, and (3) Auction Bankruptcies.

1. Firms with Released Bankruptcies. These firms were legally declared bankrupt, but during the process an agreement between the creditors and the debtor was reached. In fact, according to the law, a bankruptcy is definitively released when all the creditors agree to waive the bankruptcy or when the debtor or someone representing him decides to pay the full amount of his debts. In these cases, which were very exceptional, there have been no major losses of resources involved, because the firms have continued their operations normally.[5]

2. Firms Declared Economic Units. If proposed by the official receiver and approved by the debtor, two or more creditors, representing more than half of total liabilities, could agree to liquidate the bankrupt firm as a whole, in which case the firm was declared an "economic unit." Also, the Ministry of Finance and the Corporación de Fomento de la Producción (CORFO)[6] had the right to declare a bankrupt firm an economic unit.

However, there were no clear criteria to decide in which cases a firm could be declared an economic unit. In practice, this decision was influenced by many factors, depending on the case. Among the most important are the following: results of economic studies which determined that the value of the firm as a unit was greater than if it was sold by parts; the size of the firm, in particular, when the shutdown of a big firm left many workers unemployed; political factors and personal influence. In general, an economic unit was created when CORFO or the Ministry of Finance decided that, considering the social and economic interest of the country, it was advisable to avoid the dismantling of an industrial establishment.

In some cases, when the bankrupt firm owned more than one plant, only the most productive ones were declared economic units, the rest were dismantled and sold by parts. Also, those assets that were not directly related with the operations of the firms (gymnasiums, land, real estate, etc.) were sold.

The economic units could be of two types: with and without continuing operations. The former could be total or partial, and firms belonging to this type continued their operations after the firm was declared bankrupt.[7] When proposed by the official receiver, this decision could only be made by creditors representing no less than two-thirds of the bankruptcy liabilities, and by the unanimous decision of creditors in the case it was not proposed by the official receiver.[8] The economic units could continue their operations for no more than a year, a period that could be extended up to six months. However, in some cases (e.g. *Machasa*) this period was extended much longer.

An economic unit without continuing operations had to be bid on as a unit; however, during the bankruptcy procedure the plant was closed. In practice, these cases were quite exceptional, because most of the economic units were permitted to continue their total or partial operations during the bankruptcy procedure.

It is interesting to analyze the implications and changes associated with the functioning of the economic units. In most cases the production processes were streamlined. The economic units had to sell the assets that were not directly related to their production processes and in some cases inefficient production lines were dismantled. The idea was to concentrate production in those lines with relatively greater productivity.

Another objective behind these decisions was to increase firms' liquidity. This process was achieved by selling those assets that firms could dispense with and by discharging those workers associated with inefficient activities. Thus wage costs were reduced and operational net income was increased, which in turn reduced the need to finance working capital with short-run credits. This was a way out of the indebtedness spiral as discussed in Chapter 3 in the section on "Financial Reform: Domestic Liberalization and Opening to International Markets." However, these firms' efforts were complemented by government help, which came basically through renegotiations between the Central Bank and the private banks. This led the latter to renegotiate firms' indebtedness under more favorable conditions. In addition, government help came through direct subsidies, such as a preferential value of the dollar for all those who had debts denominated in dollars.

During the bankruptcy procedure, the economic units were prohibited by law from replacing their equipment and making investments. This was no problem for those units that were closed during the bankruptcy procedure or for those that were sold in a relatively short period of time. However, this fact became an important constraint for those firms which operated as economic units for a long period of time, since the recovery of some firms depended on the replacement of machinery or equipment.

The general information available about economic units is summarized in Table 4.1. We observe that these were relatively few compared with the total number of bankruptcies in a given year (columns 1 and 2). For instance, from a total of 431 bankrupt firms in 1981, only seven were declared economic units.[9] On the other hand, an important percentage of total economic units belonged to the manufacturing sector. (Compare columns 2 and 3 of Table 4.1.) This percentage is greater than the share of total manufacturing bankruptcies in total bankruptcies.[10]

TABLE 4.1 General Indicators on Economic Units: 1978-1982

Years	Total Number of Bankruptcies	Total Number of Economic Units	Number of Economic Units Belonging to Manufacturing	Number of Economic Units: Sold at First Bid	Number of Economic Units: Sold at Second Bid	Number of Economic Units: Without Bidders	Average Annual Sale Price: Average Annual Minimum Price (%): 1st Bid	Average Annual Sale Price: Average Annual Minimum Price (%): 2nd Bid
	(1)	(2)	(3)	(4)	(5)	(6)	(7)	(8)
1978	311	2	2	0 (a)	1 (a)	0	-	0.0
1979	344	17	11	7	5 (a)	4	19.2	14.7
1980	415	7	4	4	1	2	164.5	25.6
1981	431	7	3	3	2 (a)	1	225.4	2.6
1982	810	15	6	1 (b)	1 (b)	1	-	-
Total	2,311	48	26	15	10	8	-	-

Source: Table 2.6 and Fiscalia Nacional de Quiebras.

Notes: (a) No information available for one firm.
(b) Information available for only three firms.

However, in spite of the fact that the number of economic units was low, the size of these firms was relatively large. Considering any indicator of firm size, like number of employees and/or assets or sales, most of the economic units were among the largest of their groups.

From this information it is possible to make three important points. First, the declaration of an economic unit, the principal mechanism established by the law to avoid the dismantling of firms, was used only in very exceptional cases. Only 2.1 percent of total bankrupt firms between 1978 and 1982 were declared economic units. Second, these firms were relatively large, and third, during the period 1978–1982, more than half of the economic units (54.2 percent) belonged to the industrial sector.

The procedure used to liquidate the assets of an economic unit was the following: First, the rules for bidding were established. These rules included the quantity and quality of the assets belonging to the economic unit, as well as the minimum price, the terms, means of payment, and the collateral needed to buy the firm. If nobody was interested in bidding, the official receiver could offer it again at a lower price. This new price could not be less than two-thirds of the minimum price. If in this second opportunity there were no bidders, the economic unit could be sold under the general conditions established by the law for firms that were not declared economic units.[11]

The little information available about the economic units' bidding process is also presented in Table 4.1. The data refer to 33 economic units, out of which 18 did not have bidders in the first call; thus, a second bid had to be made for these firms. (See columns 4, 5, and 6 of Table 4.1.) As mentioned before, the price for the second bid could fluctuate between a lower limit equal to two-thirds of the set minimum price and an upper limit equal to the minimum price. However, from the interviews, it is possible to conclude that the second bid was usually very close, if not equal to, the lower limit.

In Table 4.1, we observe that 18 economic units did not have bidders in the first call, only 10 were sold in the second call and thus, eight followed the normal procedure for bankrupt firms, the third type of bankruptcy which is discussed below. In columns 7 and 8 of Table 4.1, the relationship between the selling price and the minimum price is presented. The first thing to note is that, with very few exceptions, the selling price was only slightly above the minimum price. In only six cases was the selling price significantly above the minimum price.[12] In all the rest, firms were bought at the minimum price plus 5 percent.

On the other hand, the selling price for those economic units that were sold at the first call was significantly greater than the selling price for those bid in the second call. (Compare columns 7 and 8 of Table

4.1.) Finally, the selling price did not exhibit substantial differences among those economic units that were sold in cash or in time payments. However, if we take the six firms that were sold at the highest price, five of them were sold in time payments and only one in cash.

3. Auction Bankruptcies. Most of the bankrupt firms belong to this category. The main characteristic of these firms is that their production units were dismantled and their machinery and equipment were auctioned separately. This disintegration process reduced the productive capacity of these industries, because those production lines to which the machinery and equipment belonged ceased to exist. In what follows an attempt is made to analyze this issue. The objective is to determine the destination of the machinery and equipment of these firms after the auction took place. From the interviews it was possible to identify the following cases.

The first case to be decribed is an example of those situations where the production line was sold as a unit and afterwards reinstalled in another firm on a different scale, usually smaller and more specialized. The machinery and equipment belonging to those bankrupt firms that made investments, attempting to modernize their operations to increase their level of competitiveness, were usually auctioned in this way. As analyzed in the next section, most of these firms got into debt denominated in dollars to import the required equipment and machinery. However, after the devaluation of 1982, their debts increased to unsustainable levels, resulting in their bankruptcy.[13]

Nonetheless, the machinery had already been imported. Usually the buyers for this machinery were competing firms which saw the possibility of buying relatively new and modern equipment at greatly discounted prices. This phenomenon was the result of the 1982 economic crisis which among other things, forced bankrupt firms to sell new equipment at equivalent dollar prices less than their original dollar value.

In the second case, the machinery and equipment were auctioned separately as units. Two things could happen to these assets. First, they could be dismantled to be sold as used spare parts. In fact, some people became specialists in the business of buying, dismantling and selling used parts for replacement. Second, the machinery was bought by small entrepreneurs belonging to the same manufacturing group, usually to replace their old machinery and, in some cases, to increase their production capacity. In other words, larger scale production processes were disintegrated and this capital stock was reallocated to small productive units.

The third case consists of those situations where nobody was interested in the auction and/or the buyer resold the equipment for scrap.

Finally, in a few cases, the used machinery was exported to be used in other countries.

To summarize, the destiny of the machinery and equipment auctioned took a variety of forms; nonetheless, this does not alter the two main conclusions drawn from experience with this largest category of bankrupt firms. Namely, that approximately 95 percent of all bankruptcy cases belonged to this category, and second, that in all cases, to a greater or lesser degree, the productive units were dismantled, thus reducing the productive capacity of these firms.

Reactions and Adjustments of Bankrupt Firms: Some Case Studies

The objective of this section is to take a closer look at the reactions and adjustments of bankrupt manufacturing firms. The purpose is to identify, at the firm level, the type of problems these firms faced and the different measures they took to try to overcome these problems. The emphasis is on the forms of adjustments in the operations of these firms, in particular on changes in their production strategies and in the functioning of their financial systems.

The analysis is based on 11 bankrupt cases occurring between 1979 and 1982. From interviews in 1984 with the directors of these firms, it was possible to isolate three typical patterns followed by these firms after declaring bankruptcy. The patterns reflect a composite rather than any one single firm. A fourth pattern based on interviews with four firms which survived is presented. This case will allow a contrast between the types of adjustment processes followed by bankrupt firms and those of surviving firms. The questionnaire that was used as a basis for the interviews is presented in the last part of this section.

Case 1: Adjustment by Competing in External Markets

This is the story of those bankrupt firms that tried to adjust to the new economic conditions by reorienting their sales toward external markets. These were import competing firms usually producing regular consumer goods like textiles, wearing apparel or footwear, producing mainly for the domestic market before 1974. They were medium sized, employing between 150 and 300 workers. We will assume in this first case that they were private, independently-owned corporations in the sense that they did not belong to a local economic conglomerate.

The point of departure is the recession of 1975 and the beginning of the reduction of tariffs and other trade restrictions. Both of these measures and others designed to encourage the development of exports led these firms to become more competitive and to reorient their sales to the external markets. In order to achieve this goal, these firms needed to modernize their productive structure by buying new equipment and machinery. To finance these expenditures they went into debt.

The currency denomination of these loans varies depending on the year the adjustments were made, and on the expectations entrepreneurs had about the exchange rate policy. However, these loans were normally denominated in dollars and when the loans were denominated in pesos the firms usually ended up transferring them to dollar loans. This was because the interest paid on peso loans was higher than on dollar loans. So the entrepreneurs who thought this differential was sufficient to make up for the risk of a devaluation decided to either ask for dollar loans and/or to transfer their borrowings to dollars.[14] This issue is crucial to the understanding of the severe effects of the maxi-devaluation that took place in June 1982, especially to those firms that had most of their debts denominated in dollars.

These firms needed to finance not only the purchase of new equipment but also the working capital necessary to implement these types of operations. Remember that these firms were facing an internal recession, so they did not have their own financial sources. Consequently they went to the domestic capital market for short-term working capital financing.

Around 1978 these firms began to realize that they could not compete in the external markets. On the one hand the exchange rate was already being used as an anti-inflationary device, which greatly reduced their competitiveness. On the other hand, and partly as a consequence of the former, these firms began to have serious problems paying the interest on their debts. Thus, they were forced to go further into debt at very high interest rates to fulfill their financial obligations. In some cases financial expenditures rose to 50 percent of total sales.

In an effort to overcome this situation, these firms turned to the domestic market again. At this point their financial burden was large, so they tried to sell some of their dispensable assets to reduce their liabilities. Also, those firms that had peso loans transferred their loans to dollars.

By the end of 1981 and the beginning of 1982 the economy began to show signs of the severe crisis that was to come. Production and sales began to slow down, the level of indebtedness was extraordinarily high and most of it was denominated in dollars. The level of competitiveness continued to fall as the economic authorities continued to enforce the fixed exchange rate system and the automatic adjustment mechanism. The devaluation of June 1982 was the last and final call for these firms. Their situation was extraordinarily weak and they were not able to survive a crisis of this magnitude. The rest of the story has already been told in the previous section. The firms went bankrupt, their plants were closed, and their equipment and machinery dismantled.

Case 2: Adjustment by Competing in Domestic Markets

There are two important differences between the previous case and this one. First, these firms decided to compete in the domestic markets and not to export. Second, we will assume that these firms belonged to a local economic conglomerate, or that at some point they were bought by a conglomerate. Additionally they were medium-sized import competing firms, usually producing regular consumer goods.

These firms were affected by the 1975 recession and by the liberalization of international trade. Their reaction was to reorient their domestic sales, i.e. from intermediate to finished consumer goods. In some cases they tried to reduce costs by streamlining production, better inventory management, and more efficient use of factors of production. In other cases, they tried to increase their level of competitiveness by substituting cheaper imported raw materials for more expensive domestic ones. However, these firms felt that these adjustments had to be accompanied by a modernization process mainly consisting of a combination of changes in product designs and in marketing strategies.

To finance this modernization process they went into debt. For example, one firm went into debt to buy a license to use foreign equipment and to hire U.S. technical advisers. Some firms went into debt to finance the import of raw material. At least in the beginning, most of this debt was of a short-run nature and was denominated in pesos. The ensuing loss of competitiveness led these firms to increase their debt to refinance their short-term credits. In the process, most of these firms transferred their loans to dollars, and usually sold their dispensable assets, in an attempt to reduce their heavy financial burden.

At this point these firms were in a weakened condition and the fact that they belonged to an economic conglomerate made their situation even worse. When the conglomerate went bankrupt these firms were unable to obtain more credit and they also went bankrupt. In one case, the conglomerate went bankrupt when one of its member firms still had dispensable assets to sell and, according to management, was still economically viable. This is an interesting outcome, because in the past firms benefitted from membership in a conglomerate, especially through the access to credit. But by the end of 1981 and the beginning of 1982 some firms went bankrupt earlier than would be expected, largely due to the fact that they belonged to a conglomerate.

Case 3: Adjustment Based on Favorable Expectations

This is the story of those firms which had favorable expectations and basically did not go through any adjustment process, waiting for the economic conditions to change. We will assume they were import-competing, independently-owned corporations of a medium size. We will also assume that these firms started with a manageable amount of debt.[15]

Again these firms were affected by the 1975 recession and by the opening-up to international trade. But their reaction was to wait and see what was going to happen, expecting that the new policies would not last long. In an attempt to overcome the 1975 recession and to repay their loans, these firms went further into debt, usually short-term peso loans to finance their needs for working capital. However, because things did not improve, they had to continue borrowing at extremely high interest rates. In some cases they were able to transfer their debts to dollars. In any case, the outcome for these firms was the same: unsustainable financial expenditures and severe losses in competitiveness which led finally to their bankruptcy.

Case 4: Adjustment of Firms that Survived

The adjustments followed by those firms which survived vary depending on the size and type of production of the firm and on whether they belonged to an economic conglomerate. In many cases, the adjustments these firms made were very similar to that of firms that went bankrupt. However, as I will show below, successful financial management seems to be the distinct characteristic of the firms that survived.

Because of the recession of 1975 and the opening to international trade, most of these firms went through a process of adjusting their production strategies to the new economic conditions. Their main objective was to reduce costs to become more competitive. This process was achieved through production streamlining, involving better inventory management and changes in the quality and range of goods produced. The purpose here was to reduce production lines, down to those which the firms felt were competitive with imports. Firms that were competing with imports began to import certain products themselves, products that were no longer manufactured domestically. In this way they took advantage of their inside knowledge of the market and of the distribution networks they had built for their own production.

The financial costs associated with high inventory levels, at a time when interest rates were high, led these firms to take special measures to reduce inventory size. As the process of opening the economy to international trade deepened and the competition of imports increased, some firms closed those plants that were relatively less efficient in competing with imports.

Many of the adjustments described above were also made by some of the firms that went bankrupt. However, a distinct characteristic almost always present in those firms that survived was the crucial role played by the type of financial management followed during the time of high interest rates. The most common financial maneuver, especially during the time when the exchange rate was fixed, was straightforward financial intermediation. These firms were able to increase their profits significantly by borrowing dollars in the external markets and depositing them at the high interest rates prevailing in the domestic capital market. In other words, these firms were able to take advantage of the considerable differential between the greater real cost of credit in pesos versus that in dollars.

Those firms that survived were also confronted with the decision of transferring their borrowings to dollars. In some cases they did so and they were severely affected by the devaluation of 1982. However, the measures implemented to overcome the financial crash of 1982, as discussed in the following chapter, allowed these firms to survive.

Questionnaire[16]

1. Basic Information

- Name of firm.
- Ownership (local corporation, multinational association, affiliated corporation, family firm, state firm). Has the ownership changed hands between 1974 and 1982?
- Indicators of the firm's size (sales, employment, share of imports in domestic sales).
- Explain if the three main products in your sales have changed between 1974 and 1982.

2. Basic Bankruptcy Information

- Date of bankruptcy declaration.
- Indicate who requested the bankruptcy.
- Indicate the general condition of your assets and liabilities when the bankruptcy was requested.

- Indicate to which category your firm belonged:
  (1) Firm with released bankruptcy
  (2) Declared economic unit
  (3) Declared economic unit without continuing operations
  (4) Auctioned
- In cases (2), (3) and (4) above please describe the bankruptcy procedure followed in your case.
- Describe the procedure used to liquidate the assets of the firm. Try to identify the general condition of the machinery and equipment of your firm at the moment of the liquidation.
- How long was the bankruptcy process?

3. Adjustments to Economic Changes

Please comment on the importance to your firm of the following economic changes:

- Increase in the cost of working capital.
- Increase in external competition due to the reduction of restrictions on imports.
- Increase in external competition in the domestic market due to the appreciation of the peso.
- Decrease in the earning power of exports due to the lower dollar value of export products.
- Decrease in the earning power of exports due to the appreciation of the peso.
- Increase in the price of domestic raw material, proportionally greater than in the price of the product.
- Better access to fixed capital financing.
- Better opportunities to buy foreign machinery and equipment not available before.
- Increase in export opportunities.

4. Adjustments in the Operation of the Firm

Please indicate the relative importance of the following adjustments in terms of their impact on your profits:

- Changes in the area of activities, e.g. began to import or to engage in money lending.
- Changes in the diversification of production.
- Changes in inventory policy.
- Plant closings and/or production streamlining.
- Changes in product quality.

- Changes in vertical integration.

Regarding marketing and financial adjustments:

- Changes in marketing strategy.
- Changes in financial control.
- Net change in assets.
- Net change in liabilities.
- Increase in investment.

5. Diversification of Activities

Regarding imports and/or assembly and distribution:

- Access to or ownership of a chain of distribution.
- Previous contact with foreign sellers.
- Possession of import license, which gave the firm an advantage.
- Changes in earnings due to the intermediation of commercial financing.

Regarding financial activities:

- Availability of liquid assets.
- Changes to activities in which the consumer requires substantial financing.

6. Market Characteristics

- Indicate how your firm compares with your competitors in terms of product prices and quality, scale of production, marketing and distribution, organization of production, and financial management.
- Indicate the changes that occurred with domestic and foreign competition. (Identify these changes by major products.)
- Regarding pricing decisions, which of the following factors were important to your firm:
  1. Maintain market share
  2. Cost of capital and raw material
  3. Domestic competition
  4. Import competition

Notes

1. *Diário Oficial* (Official Newspaper) of Chile, October 28, 1982.

2. From an interview with a lawyer of the Fiscalia Nacional de Quiebras (Government Agency of Bankruptcies).

3. See Title IX of the Law 18.175 of October 1982.

4. See Title VIII of the Law 18.175 of October 1982.

5. Three examples of this type are: Firestone, *Compañia Industrial* and *Constructora Cerrillos.*

6. It is a public office under the Finance Ministry, which owns and manages some of the most important public enterprises.

7. Some Economic Units with continuing operations were *Manufactura Chilena de Algodon (Machasa); VESTEX, TOME; Paños TOME; Fabrica de Cerrajerias y Pernos Ferromat* and *Distribuidora Industrial Nacional (DIN).* IRT is a case with partially continuing operations. Compañia Industrial and Constructora Cerrillos are cases of economic units where the bankruptcies were released after an agreement was reached.

8. Law 18.175, article 112.

9. Of these seven, only three belonged to the manufacturing sector: *Malteria Aconcagua; Fabrica de Cerrajerias y Pernos Ferromat* and *Machasa.* The other four were *Soc. Promotora Servicio de Salud Ltd.; Cia. Minera Delirio de Punitaqui S.A.; Comercializadora Automotriz del Norte S.A.* and *Distribudora Industrial Nacional (DIN).*

10. See Table 2.7 in Chapter 2.

11. See section on "Auction Bankruptcies" in this chapter.

12. During 1979: *SOLECHE Ltd.* and *Establecimientos Metalurgicos INDAC S.A.* During 1980: *UNICOOP Ltd.; Soc. Minera SAGASCA S.A.* and *SEC Ingenieria.* During 1981: *ENAGAS.*

13. *Scapini Industrial S.A.* is a case in point. In 1977 they decided to make investments in order to export. To buy the new equipment they got into debt denominated in dollars. With the devaluation of 1982 their financial burden increased to unsustainable levels and in October 1982 they went bankrupt.

14. The expectations of devaluations played a crucial role in the financial management of manufacturing firms. Apparently, at the beginning of the period after the exchange rate was fixed, the expectations of a devaluation were high. Then they declined, but rose again at the end of 1981 and during the first semester of 1982.

15. Typical cases of indebted firms in 1974–1975 were those that were sold by the government to the private sector. The shares of these firms were bought on two or three year loans. The buyers expected no problems in paying this debt, assuming that the firms would operate normally.

16. Adapted from PREALC (1984) and Corbo and Sanchez (1984).

5

Characteristics of the Industrial Recovery: 1983–1986

The main objective of this chapter is to analyze the performance of the industrial sector during the period of economic recovery, i.e. 1983–1986. The idea is to see if the new information available can help us to better understand the magnitude of the the deindustrialization process. In other words, we want to analyze whether the transformations which occurred during the recovery can deepen our understanding of the deindustrialization period.

The Macroeconomic Context

The year 1982 was a breaking point for industry in Chile. The severe recession of 1982 (industrial output decreased by 21.6 percent that year) was the clearest evidence of the failure of the economic model imposed since 1974.

The recovery after the 1982 recession was accompanied by changes in economic policies, which had a positive impact on the growth rate of all productive sectors. In fact, the growth structure among economic sectors changed substantially after 1982. During the period 1975–1981 the leading economic sectors were the commercial and financial sectors. After the 1982 recession the goods-producing sectors became the leaders, especially industry.

The causes of these changes are found in the persistent and inflexible orthodoxy with which the monetary model of the balance of payments was applied between 1979 and 1982. This situation intensified the effects of the 1982 recession much more than was necessary. The extreme decrease in output and employment could have been avoided if corrective measures had been taken in time. Instead, the economic authorities of that time insisted on continuing to apply their economic model.[1] The year 1982 corresponds to an extraordinary nadir in the economic cycle. Thus, because it would have been nearly impossible to sink further, it is not surprising that in 1983 Chilean industry began a recovery.

Two principal changes in the economic policy were introduced in the last quarter of 1982. In the first place, relative prices changed in favor of the tradable sectors, leading to recovering the industrial competitiveness which had been lost. In the second place, an active fiscal policy was implemented, particularly in the construction of public infrastructure and housing.

Regarding the changes in relative prices, the exchange rate policy changed from a fixed to a passive crawling-peg system. First a maxi-devaluation was implemented and then a policy of daily devaluation (based on past inflation minus an estimation of international inflation) was put into effect. At the same time, tariffs increased from 10 percent to 20 percent across the board. Few products were exempt from this rule and in these cases an overtariff was applied.

On the financial front, measures were taken to ease the burden on domestic debtors. A preferential exchange rate was created for those who had debts in dollars above a certain level. This measure was equivalent to granting a subsidy equal to the difference between the official and the preferential exchange rate. An indirect mechanism was implemented for those with debts in Chilean pesos. The Central Bank decided to first alleviate the situation of private banks since the majority of them were technically bankrupt. The most important private banks in the country were taken over by the Government. The Central Bank purchased the past-due loans of the banks with the agreement that they would re-purchase those loans, paying a certain proportion each year. This measure permitted some firms to re-negotiate their debt with the banks under more favorable conditions. Also, selective re-negotiation policies, according to the level of indebtedness, were established for those debtors in domestic currency. However, in spite of these measures, in 1986 the internal debt continued to be one of the most serious problems obstructing the development of industry in Chile.

There are two other factors which were helpful in the post-1982 recovery of industry. First, the big reduction in real wages, together with the measures described above, led to a recovery of the level of profitability for those firms with exporting activities, which also benefitted from the changes in the exchange rate policy. Second, state enterprises changed their policy of buying intermediate goods, substituting domestically produced inputs for imported ones.

As we will see in the next sections, the recovery of Chilean industry was based primarily on import substitution and on the recovery of internal demand, particularly from increases in the demand from the

TABLE 5.1 Industrial GDP According to National Accounts (percentages)

	Share of Industry in Total GDP		Annual Rate of Growth	
	(1)	(2)	(3)	(4)
1970	24.7	25.5	-	-
1980	21.6	20.9	6.2	2.4
1981	20.9	19.7	2.6	-1.3
1982	19.3	19.6	-21.0	-13.9
1983	20.0	20.3	3.1	2.8
1984	20.7	20.9	9.8	11.9
1985	20.4	21.1	1.2	1.6
1986	20.8	-	8.0	-
Average				
1960-70	24.1	25.2	5.3	5.5
1974-86	21.4	21.5 (a)	0.6	-0.6 (a)
1974-81	22.1	22.0	1.4	-1.0
1982-85	20.1	20.5	4.6	5.4
1982-86	20.2	-	5.4	-

Sources: Columns 2 and 4: MARCEL, M. and MELLER, P. "Empalme de las cuentas nacionales de Chile 1960-1985. Metodos alternativos y resultados" in Coleccion Estudios CIEPLAN No. 20, Santiago, Diciembre, 1986.
Columns 1 and 3: Banco Central de Chile, Cuentas Nacionales.

Note: (a) Average 1974-1985.

construction sector for intermediate goods. Another effect, although less important, was the increase in exporting activities such as mining.

The Evolution of Employment and Industrial Output

In this section we analyze aggregate indicators of employment and industrial output in order to have an overall view of the performance of the industrial sector after the 1982 crisis.

Let us consider first the evolution of industrial output. In Table 5.1 we present the national account figures calculated by the Central Bank (columns 1 and 3) and the ones estimated by Marcel and Meller (1986) (columns 2 and 4).[2] Even though since 1983 there are important differences between these sources, both show that the industrial sector has gone through a process of recovery. The average annual growth rate during the period 1982–1985 varies between 4.6 percent (Central Bank) and 5.4 percent (Marcel and Meller, 1986). For the period 1982–

TABLE 5.2 Index of Industrial Production According to Industrial Surveys (percentages)

	INE (1979=100)	SOFOFA (a) (1969=100)	SOFOFA (b) (1980=100)
1980	100.0	100.0	100.1
1981	100.8	100.1	100.7
1982	84.6	82.5	86.4
1983	88.7	86.3	89.5
1984	97.6	93.6	98.7
1985	97.7	93.0	98.8
1986	105.5	100.7	106.8
Average Annual Growth Rate			
1982-85	4.9	4.1	4.6
1982-86	5.7	5.1	5.4

Source: INE, Indice de Produccion Industrial Manufacturera and SOFOFA, Indice de Produccion Industrial.

Notes: (a) Old Index with weights of 1969.
(b) New Index with weights of 1979.

1986 we only have the official figures which indicate an average annual growth rate of 5.4 percent.

Considering the overall pattern it is important to note that the official figures estimated a reduction in industrial GDP in 1982 much greater than the revised figures of Marcel and Meller (1986), 21.0 percent versus 13.9 percent respectively. Afterwards, according to the Central Bank, industry recovered at lower rates than the ones estimated by Marcel and Meller (1986).

In Table 5.2 we present the output industrial index according to the industrial surveys made by the *Instituto Nacional de Estadística* (INE) and the *Sociedad de Fomento Fabril* (SOFOFA). In 1980, the latter changed the weights of its index to ones that correspond to the 1979 National Manufacturing Census. Therefore in Table 5.2 we present SOFOFA's old index (1960=100) and new index (1980=100).

The results do not vary substantially for the period 1982–1986. The average annual growth rate varies between 5.1 percent (old SOFOFA) and 5.7 percent (INE). Also, according to the Central Bank, the average annual growth rate for the period 1982–1986 (5.4 percent) is equal to the one estimated by the new index of SOFOFA.

In Table 5.1 columns (1) and (2), we show that the recovery has increased the share of industrial output in total GDP, according to both sources of information. However, this indicator continues to be much smaller than the one in the 1960s. The average for the 1982–1986 period was 20.2 percent compared to 24.1 percent during 1960–1970.

The main conclusion is that, according to the existing sources, the industrial sector recovered at an average annual rate of around 5.4 percent during 1982–1986, generating about one-fifth of total GDP.

Let us consider now the evolution of industrial employment. In Table 5.3 we present the available figures according to three alternative sources: the University of Chile, INE, and Jadresic (1986). These three sources can only be compared for the period 1982–1985 because the Jadresic (1986) figures were only estimated up to 1985.

For this period, the University of Chile and Jadresic (1986) estimated an average annual growth rate of 5.1 percent and INE a considerably larger rate of 9.2 percent. The reason for this difference is that according to INE, industrial employment decreased in 1982 by 27.5 percent and according to the University of Chile and Jadresic (1986), it decreased by 21.0 and 18.6 percent respectively.

According to these two latter sources, employment in 1983 continued to decrease at rates which fluctuated between 3.2 and 4.2 percent. However, according to INE, industrial employment in 1983 recovered at a rate of 8.5 percent. This rate is certainly somewhat high, especially compared to the rate of growth of output that year, which according to INE was 4.8 percent. Additional figures according to INE industrial surveys of establishments of 10 or more employees show that industrial employment decreased in 1983 at a rate of 2.1 percent.

Thus, considering the information given by different sources it is possible to conclude that INE overestimated the reduction of industrial employment in 1982 and the increase in 1983, all of which determined an upward bias in INE's estimations for the period 1982–1985.

The University of Chile is the only source that gives comparable figures for the period 1982–1986. The INE figures are not comparable because those beginning in the quarter November 1985–January 1986 correspond to a new sample. The University of Chile gives an average annual rate of 8.7 percent. However, this rate is somewhat overestimated because the University of Chile estimated an increase of 15.8 percent for the year 1986. (See Table 5.3.)

This figure is relatively high considering that industrial output increased by 8.0 percent and employment, according to the new INE survey, by 8.7 percent. If we assume that during 1986 industrial employment increased at this latter rate, i.e. 8.7 percent, the average annual growth rate for the period 1982–1986 would have fluctuated between 6.0 percent, according to Jadresic (1986), and 7.0 percent, according to the University of Chile.

TABLE 5.3 Industrial Employment According to Different Sources (percentages)

	Universidad de Chile			Jadresic (1986)			INE		
	Share in Total Employment		Annual Growth Rate	Share in Total Employment		Annual Growth Rate	Share in Total Employment		Annual Growth Rate
	With EEP(a)	Without EEP		With EEP	Without EEP		With EEP	Without EEP	
1980	17.3	18.3	-	15.3	16.2	-	16.1	17.2	-
1981	16.6	17.5	-1.0	14.4	15.2	-1.7	15.8	16.7	-1.5
1982	14.4	15.5	-21.0	12.9	14.1	-18.6	12.7	14.6	-27.5
1983	14.0	16.2	-3.2	11.7	13.9	-4.2	12.6	14.9	8.5
1984	14.5	16.1	14.6	12.8	14.2	14.3	13.8	15.5	14.2
1985	15.0	16.5	8.6	12.9	14.2	6.0	13.8	15.0	5.1
1986	16.4	17.5	15.8	-	-	-	13.6(b)	14.3(b)	8.7(c)
Average									
1982-85	14.5	16.1	5.1	12.6	14.1	5.1	13.2	15.0	9.2
1982-86	14.9	16.4	8.7	-	-	-	-	-	-
1974-85	-	-	-	-	-	-1.5	-	-	-

Sources: Universidad de Chile, "Ocupacion y Desocupacion. Encuesta Nacional" Santiago, Septiembre, 1985.

Jadresic E. "Evolucion del empleo y desempleo en Chile, 1970-85", series anuales y trimestrales, in Coleccion de Estudios CIEPLAN No. 20, Santiago, Diciembre, 1986.

INE, Encuesta Nacional de Empleo. Last Quarter of each year. 1982 corresponds to October-November.

Notes: (a) EEP (Emergency Employment Programs) includes the Minimum Employment Program (PEM) and the Employment Program for Heads of Families (POJH).
(b) The year 1986 is not comparable to the rest because INE changed the sample of the survey.
(c) Average of two quarters (Dec. 1985 - Feb. 1986 and Nov. 1986 - Jan. 1987).

For the period 1982–1985 the share of industry in total employment (without emergency employment programs) fluctuated between 14.1 percent (Jadresic, 1986) and 16.1 percent (University of Chile). Even though this indicator has been recovering since 1982, in 1986 it was still below the levels reached in 1980–1981 and considerably below the levels of 1970–1971 (21.0 percent).

Summing up, during the period 1982–1985, industrial employment increased at an average annual rate of 5.1 percent. During 1982–1986 this rate fluctuated between 6.0 and 7.0 percent, depending on the source of information. Finally, by 1986, the industrial sector was generating about one-sixth of total employment.

The Role of Industry During Periods of Recovery

In this section we give additional information regarding the role of the manufacturing sector during the recovery. For this purpose, we estimated the elasticity of industrial output/total output during the 1982–1986 period and compared these results with the ones obtained during the recovery of 1975–1978. The objective is to show that after the 1982 crisis, the industrial sector played an even more important role than it played in the recovery after the 1975 recession. We observe these results in Table 5.4, line 1. Between 1975 and 1978 the industrial sector grew between 0.8 and 1.5 times for each percentage point of GDP, depending on the sources of information. Between 1982 and 1986 the growth rate of industry was between 1.7 and 1.9 times greater than the growth of total GDP.

This situation is explained mainly by two factors. In the first place, after 1975 an accelerated process of opening the economy to international trade began, with negative consequences for those import-substituting industrial sectors.[3] The opposite occurred after 1982, because tariffs were raised, the peso was devalued, and the exchange rate policy changed from a fixed to a passive crawling-peg system with the objective of maintaining a realistic real exchange rate. In the second place, after 1975 a very restrictive fiscal policy was implemented, public expenditures decreased, and the fiscal deficit was rapidly eliminated. After 1982 a relatively expansionary fiscal policy was implemented and both public expenditures and the fiscal deficit increased.

As mentioned before, the recovery of industry after 1982 was the result of economic policies which increased the levels of internal demand, policies which alleviated the burden on the financial system, and policies which changed the relative prices in favor of the tradable

TABLE 5.4 The Importance of Industry During Periods of Economic Recovery (percentages)

	1975-1978	1982-1986
1. Output		
Elasticity Industrial Output/Total Output		
1.1 Banco Central	1.1	1.7
		1.5(a)
1.2 Marcel and Meller (1986)	0.8	1.9(b)
1.3 SOFOFA	1.5	1.7
1.4 INE	1.0	1.7
2. Employment		
Elasticity Industrial Employment/ Industrial Output		
2.1 Universidad de Chile/INE	-	1.5
2.2 Universidad de Chile/SOFOFA	-	1.7
2.3 INE/INE	0.3	1.9(b)
2.4 INE/SOFOFA	0.2	2.2(b)
2.5 Marcel-Meller/Jadresic	-0.002	0.9(b)

Source: Tables 5.1, 5.2 and 5.3.

Notes: (a) Period 1982-1987. Output for 1987 is an estimation made by the Central Bank.
(b) Period 1982-1985.

sector. Particularly important was the change in the exchange rate policy which restored industrial competitiveness.

The recovery of industrial production was accompanied by an increase in the capacity of the sector to create employment. In line 2 of Table 5.4 we present different estimations of industrial employment/output elasticity, comparing the two recoveries. All of them show that employment/output elasticity increased during the period 1982–1986 compared to the period 1975–1978.

In light of these indicators, it is interesting to analyze the importance of the industrial sector in the creation of employment and the effect on output in the Chilean economy. The shrinkage of the industrial sector, produced by the neoconservative policies, is one of the main reasons explaining the high and persistant unemployment rate observed between 1974 and 1983. During the decade of the 1960s the manufacturing sector contributed in an important way to creating new employment opportunities. However, during the monetarist experiment, the industrial sector not only decreased its rate of employment absorption, but reduced the number of jobs in absolute terms. Most of these workers did not have other opportunities other than lengthening the unemployment line.

There is a final point that is important to keep in mind when analyzing the figures of employment/output elasticities of Table 5.4. If we compare the effects of the 1975 and the 1982 recessions on employment and industrial output, we see that the reduction in output in 1975 was much larger than in 1982. However, the effects on employment were the opposite, i.e. in 1975 employment decreased much less than in 1982. Hence, this could partly explain the increase in industrial employment/output elasticity during the recent recovery.[4]

The Performance of Maximum Capacity Output and the Degree of Capacity Utilization

In this section we analyze two characteristics related to the structure of industrial supply. In the first place, we estimate the evolution of productive capacity using maximum capacity output as a proxy. In the second place, we estimate the average degree of capacity utilization during the year 1986.[5] The methodology used for these estimations is the same that was used in Chapter 2. What we do here is update the estimations using the new information available.

The results are presented in Table 5.5. We observe that for total industry, maximum capacity output decreased by 2.5 percent between the periods 1974–1981 and 1982–1986. If we compare this latter period (1982–1986) with 1969–1973, this same indicator increases by 6.6 percent. Considering that we are referring to a period of approximately 10 years, this increase represents an average annual rate of only 0.64 percent, which is an extraordinarily low rate.

If we exclude the "Non-Ferrous Metal Industries" sector from total industry,[6] we observe with greater clarity the productive lag that the Chilean industrial sector has suffered. The results of Table 5.5 suggest that between 1969–1973 and 1982–1986, the aggregate productive capacity of Chilean industry fell by approximately 2 percent. If we compare the period 1974–1981 with 1982–1986, the reduction reaches 4.5 percent. As we analyze in the next section, these results are aggregate estimates and do not necessarily show what occurred in some particular sectors. Undoubtedly, some sectors increased and modernized their plants and equipment and others gradually deteriorated. In spite of this, the aggregate results show the relative magnitude of these two effects and thus the average degree of improvement of productive capacity. The results for Chile suggest that during the last 15 years, industrial productive capacity remained stagnant.

TABLE 5.5 Evolution of Maximum Capacity Output in the Chilean Manufacturing Sector, 1969-1986, and Estimation of Utilized Capacity in 1987

	Share of Total Value-Added	Maximum Capacity Output			Effective Production	Evolution of Maximum Capacity Output		Utilized Capacity
		1969-73 (1)	1974-81 (2)	1982-86 (3)	(4)	(3)/(1) (%)	(3)/(2) (%)	(3)/(4) (%)
A. Regular Consumer Goods								
Food	16.3	118.4	134.0	161.3	158.9	36.2	16.0	98.5
Beverage	5.1	132.2	166.8	150.7	131.9	14.0	-9.7	87.5
Textiles	10.2	130.0	103.7	149.1	147.4	14.7	43.8	98.9
Wearing Apparel	2.9	123.5	99.4	81.7	77.5	-33.8	-17.8	94.9
Leather	1.1	108.5	86.2	53.9	34.1	-50.3	-37.5	63.3
Footwear	1.8	134.1	85.9	64.4	58.7	-52.0	-25.0	91.1
Other Chemical Products	4.8	134.1	141.8	148.2	142.1	10.5	4.5	95.9
Subtotal	42.2	125.4	127.8	143.2	137.8	14.2	12.1	96.2
B. Durable Consumer Goods								
Machinery except Elect.	3.2	128.7	53.3	32.3	28.8	-74.9	-39.4	89.2
Communication Equip. & Apparatus	2.0	200.7	201.3	96.7	79.7	-51.8	-52.0	82.4
Elect. Appliances & Housewares	1.8	138.4	263.0	132.4	124.7	-4.3	-49.0	94.2
Subtotal	7.0	151.8	149.5	76.4	68.0	-49.7	-48.9	89.0

C. Manufacturing of Transport Equip.								
Transport Equipment	6.2	118.5	117.6	64.7	43.4	-45.4	-45.0	67.1
Subtotal	6.2	118.5	117.6	64.7	43.4	-45.4	-45.0	67.1
D. Intermediate Goods for Manufac.								
Industrial Chemicals	2.7	123.1	75.9	55.3	55.1	-55.1	-27.1	99.6
Petroleum Refineries	1.6	137.6	137.9	118.5	110.3	-13.9	-14.1	93.1
Misc. Petroleum & Coal	0.2	135.0	98.9	122.7	107.5	-9.1	24.1	87.6
Iron & Steel Basic Indust.	3.4	115.3	107.9	109.7	103.0	-4.9	1.7	93.9
Non-Ferrous Metal Indust.	13.1	130.9	197.8	210.5	208.0	60.8	6.4	98.8
Subtotal	21.0	127.9	162.1	166.4	162.9	30.1	2.7	97.9
E. Intermediate Goods for Construc.								
Wood & Cork except Furniture	3.0	155.5	220.0	189.8	175.3	22.1	-13.7	92.4
Furniture and Fixtures	1.0	140.8	223.5	226.9	225.4	61.2	1.5	99.3
Pottery, China & Earthenware	0.5	117.7	104.8	62.2	59.8	-47.2	-40.6	96.1
Glass and Glass Products	0.8	140.3	177.5	203.9	194.3	45.3	14.9	95.3
Other Non-Metallic Products	1.9	118.5	123.2	97.7	89.6	-17.6	-20.7	91.7
Fabricated Metal Products	4.3	126.8	112.8	93.9	93.1	-25.9	-16.8	99.1
Elect. Industrial Machinery	1.0	132.5	291.1	184.0	156.3	38.9	-36.8	84.9
Subtotal	12.5	134.5	167.5	141.1	133.1	4.9	-15.8	94.3

(continued)

Table 5.5 (continued)

	Share of Total Value-Added	Maximum Capacity Output			Effective Production	Evolution of Maximum Capacity Output		Utilized Capacity
		1969-73 (1)	1974-81 (2)	1982-86 (3)	(4)	(3)/(1) (%)	(3)/(2) (%)	(3)/(4) (%)
F. Miscellaneous Manufacturing Goods								
Paper and Paper Products	2.1	107.2	129.1	137.7	134.2	28.5	6.7	97.5
Printing and Publishing	2.7	156.3	117.8	97.1	74.2	-37.9	-17.6	76.4
Rubber Products	1.6	144.7	114.9	144.1	131.4	-0.4	25.4	91.2
Plastic Products	1.3	127.9	126.1	138.8	135.1	8.5	10.1	97.3
Professional Equipment	0.2	114.5	62.1	71.6	70.9	-37.5	15.3	99.0
Other Manufact. Industries	3.2	125.9	163.7	177.2	143.8	40.7	8.2	81.2
Subtotal	11.1	132.5	132.7	139.1	120.9	5.0	4.8	86.9
Total Manufacturing	100.0	129.3	141.3	137.8	129.9	6.6	-2.5	94.3
Total Manufacturing w/o group Non-Ferrous Metal Industries	-	129.1	132.8	126.8	-	-1.8	-4.5	-

Note: The estimation procedure is explained in "The Evolution of Industrial Productive Capacity: 1969-1983," Chapter 2.

In Table 5.5 we also present an estimate of the level of capacity utilization during 1986. Two points stand out from the figures. In the first place, the industrial sector is working at very low idle capacity levels. According to our estimates, in 1986 the degree of capacity utilization reached 94 percent. In the second place, this high degree of utilization was relatively homogeneous among industrial sectors.

This is an important conclusion because the estimate for 1984 (using the same methodology) showed that, in spite of the fact that the industrial sector was working at low levels of idle capacity, its distribution among sectors was very heterogeneous. Apparently, the recovery of the manufacturing sector has intensively used the spaces of idle capacity created during the crisis of 1982. This situation has important implications for the future, especially with respect to the level of investment necessary to maintain the growth rates observed during the recovery.

The Recovery of the Industrial Groups that Deteriorated Most During 1975–1982

In the "Conclusions" section of Chapter 2, we presented a summary of "deindustrialization indicators" disaggregated by manufacturing groups. Based on this information we defined those groups which were relatively more affected by the deindustrialization process. In this section we analyze the performance of these manufacturing groups during the recovery. The objective is to use the new information available to evaluate to what extent these groups were affected.

There is an important point to keep in mind when analyzing the results. There is a difference between deterioration of productive capacity and changes in production due to the economic cycle. In particular, it is possible that some groups had experienced reductions in their productive capacity during the period 1974–1982 and increases in their output during the recovery (1983–1986). In other words, it is difficult to differentiate during a severe economic crisis, such as the one of 1982, how much of the decline in output was due to reductions in productive capacity and how much to reductions in production caused by the recession. For instance, in some groups we observe that maximum capacity output decreased between 1969–1973 and 1982–1986; however, these same groups had relatively high growth rates during the recovery. This situation means that in spite of the deterioration in productive capacity, production decreased during the 1982 crisis at levels much lower than those that would have been possible if capacity had been at full employment. Thus, when the recovery began in the last quarter of 1983, firms were able to increase production due to the existing idle capacity. However, because of the deteriorated productive capacity, the existing idle capacity was rapidly utilized. This situation points to the need to increase investment to avoid this kind of bottleneck.

In Table 5.6 we present the relevant figures. In column 1 we show the evolution of maximum capacity output during three different periods: 1969–1973, 1974–1981 and 1982–1986. We observe that in 1982–1986 all the groups that we analyze below, with the single exception of Textiles, maximum capacity output was even below the already deteriorated capacity of the 1974–1981 period. In other words, as shown in Chapter 2, the economic policies implemented during the neoconservative period affected relatively more the productive capacities of these manufacturing groups. Apparently, this was an important constraint for these groups during the recovery, as evidenced by the fact that during 1982–1986 they were unable to reach the already deteriorated capacity levels of the period 1974–1981. Furthermore, most of these groups have maximum capacity outputs that are even lower that the ones existing during 1969–1973. Thus, these groups suffered irrecoverable losses in their productive capacity, as evidenced by the fact that after four years of recovery their maximum capacity outputs remained substantially lower than the average for total industry.

However, this general tendency has some peculiarities that stand out. In the first place, consider the case of the groups Communication Equipment, Transport Equipment, and Electrical Appliances and Housewares. In the first two groups maximum capacity output remained stagnant between the periods 1969–1973 and 1974–1981. The latter group even increased its capacity during this period. However, the three were severely affected by the 1982 crisis. Their maximum capacity output decreased by 54.9 percent in the case of Communication Equipment, 45 percent in the case of Transport Equipment, and 49.7 percent in the case of Electrical Appliances and Housewares.

In the second place, take the case of the group Professional Equipment. This group deteriorated severely during the neoconservative period (maximum capacity output decreased by 45.8 percent during 1974–1981). However, during the recovery it was able to exceed the level of 1974–1981. This is a case of relative recovery, because the levels of 1982–1986 are substantially lower than those of the period 1969–1973. In other words, this group has only partially recovered from the deteriorated levels of 1974–1981.

Finally we have the exceptional case of Textiles. The textile sector was severely affected by the neoconservative policies. It is my view that this is the only case in which enough evidence exists to hypothesize that this group went through a process of reconversion of its productive capacity, which allowed its remarkable recovery at extraordinarily high rates. Its maximum capacity output increased by 43.8 percent between the periods 1974–1981 and 1982–1986. Moreover, the level of this latter period was much higher than the one of 1969–1973. On the other hand, we observe in Table 5.6 that during the recovery this group had extremely high growth rates. The average annual rate reached 17 percent, much greater than the average for total industry which was 5.1 percent. This high growth rate determined that, according to the SOFOFA (1969=100) production index, in 1986 textile production was 61.6 percent greater than in 1981 and 17.6 percent greater than the historical peak recorded in 1972.

In column 8 of Table 5.6 we show that in 1984 employment in textiles grew at 10.4 percent, similar to the average for total industry (10.2 percent). Even though the information available regarding employment figures is still very scarce (the INE annual industrial surveys were only published until 1984) it is interesting to observe that the short-run employment/output elasticity in textiles in 1984 was 0.4 compared to an elasticity of 1.0 for total industry. These results show that productivity has been increasing in this sector, probably due to the incorporation of new technology. In spite of these technological changes the high degree of utilized capacity under which this group is operating poses a serious constraint for its future expansion. Table 5.6, column 2 shows that textile firms are working at levels very near full employment.

To summarize, based on the performance of the textile sector during the recovery of 1983–1986, it is possible to hypothesize that a process of reconversion occurred in those textile firms which survived. The experience of some big firms seems to confirm this hypothesis; however, the evidence available is still insufficient for definite conclusions. An interesting line of future research would be to do case studies at the firm level, to identify the changes which accounted for the rapid recovery of this sector.

Continuing with the analysis of the other groups included in Table 5.6, it is interesting to note in columns 3, 4 and 5 that in 1986, with the exception of Textiles, Fabricated Metal Products, and Professional Equipment, the rest of the groups had output levels much lower than those of 1981. This is in spite of the fact that some of these groups experienced relatively high growth rates during the recovery.

The groups Fabricated Metal Products and Professional Equipment recovered the output level of 1981; however in both cases, this latter level is much lower than the one of the 1970s. For instance, the production level of Professional Equipment in 1981 was 50 percent lower than its 1971 historical annual peak. In other words, in these

TABLE 5.6 Post-Crisis Performance of Manufacturing Sectors Which Were Relatively More Deteriorated During 1974-1982

Groups	Evolution of Maximum Capacity Output (1)			Utilized Capacity in 1986 (2)	Annual Growth Rate (3)				
	1969-73	1974-81	1982-86	1986	1982	1983	1984	1985	1986
A. Regular Goods									
Textiles	130.0	103.7	149.1	98.9	-13.7	26.3	19.8	1.1	22.4
Wearing Apparel	123.5	99.4	81.7	94.9	-17.1	1.8	18.6	-6.5	3.3
Leather	108.5	86.2	53.9	63.3	-23.4	-6.7	-6.6	-9.9	-18.6
Footwear	134.1	85.9	64.4	91.1	-20.4	8.6	-6.4	-3.4	7.3
B. Durable Goods									
Machinery except Electric	128.7	53.3	32.3	89.2	-34.0	-19.1	12.2	1.1	7.1
Communication Equip. & Apparatus	200.7	201.3	90.7	82.4	-59.1	-28.0	25.2	-13.6	28.1
Elect. Appliances and Houseware	138.4	263.0	132.4	94.2	-60.9	-8.7	39.7	-25.2	46.7

C. Intermediate Goods for Construction									
Fabricated Metal Products	126.8	112.8	93.9	99.1	-26.7	4.3	14.3	0.5	14.0
D. Manuf. of Transport Equip.									
Transport Equipment	118.5	117.6	64.7	67.1	-37.1	-28.2	-1.6	22.1	-15.4
E. Miscellaneous Goods									
Professional Equipment	114.5	62.1	71.6	99.0	-38.3	25.2	10.4	12.5	38.2
Total Manufacturing	129.3	141.3	137.8	94.3	-17.6	4.6	8.4	-0.6	8.2
Total Manuf. w/o group Non-Ferrous Metal Indust.	129.1	132.8	126.8	-	-	-	-	-	-

(continued)

Table 5.6 (continued)

Groups	Average Annual Growth Rate		Output 1986/1981	Structure of Value Added		Number of Establishments			Employment		
	1982-86	1981-86	(%)	1969	1979	1982	1983	1984	1982	1983	1984
	(4)		(5)	(6)		(7)			(8)		
A. Regular Goods											
Textiles	17.0	10.1	161.1	10.2	5.4	350	327	336	18,889	19,796	21,850
Wearing Apparel	3.9	-0.7	96.8	2.9	2.7	305	265	294	12,654	10,603	12,914
Leather	-10.6	-13.3	48.9	1.1	0.8	59	53	51	2,469	2,109	2,229
Footwear	1.3	-3.5	83.9	1.8	1.7	127	127	133	6,809	6,971	8,177
B. Durable Goods											
Machinery except Electric	-0.4	-8.3	64.9	3.2	2.1	138	125	133	8,755	9,096	9,527
Communication Equip. & Apparatus	-0.1	-16.4	40.8	2.0	0.1	-	-	-	-	-	-
Elect. Appliances and Houseware	8.7	-11.4	54.6	1.8	0.4	57(a)	55	59	3,737	3,418	3,702

C. Intermediate Goods for Construction											
Fabricated Metal Products	8.1	0.0	100.0	4.3	4.3	365	322	358	16,620	13,720	16,544
D. Manuf. of Transport Equip.											
Transport Equipment	-7.6	-14.4	45.9	6.2	3.4	94	87	83	5,039	3,864	4,568
E. Miscellaneous Goods											
Professional Equipment	21.1	5.8	132.5	0.2	0.1	15	15	14	513	381	473
Total Manufacturing	5.1	0.1	100.6	-	-	4,130	4,205	4,378	223,138	218,532	240,885
Total Manuf. w/o group Non-Ferrous Metal Indust.	-	-	-	-	-	-	-	-	-	-	-

Sources: Columns 1 and 2: Table 5.5
Columns 3, 4 and 5: SOFOFA (1969=100).
Column 6: INE: Industrial Census.
Columns 7 and 8: INE: Annual Industrial Surveys.

TABLE 5.7 Leading Industrial Sectors During the Recovery of 1983-1986

	Average Annual Growth Rates		
	1975-78	1975-81	1982-86
Category A			
Textiles	10.8	4.8	19.7
Elect. Appliances & Housewares	25.9	22.1	21.7
Rubber Products	22.7	13.6	20.1
Professional Equipment	-4.0	-1.0	20.5
Category B			
Wood & Cork except Furniture	34.6	19.9	10.1
Furniture and Fixtures	16.8	20.9	17.2
Pottery, China & Earthenware	8.4	0.6	26.0
Glass and Glass Products	39.2	18.5	20.1
Other Non-Metallic Products	6.4	11.3	12.4
Category C			
Industrial Chemicals	8.0	0.9	11.8
Misc. Petroleum & Coal	13.2	6.8	11.7

Source: SOFOFA: Indice de Produccion Industrial. The period 1982-1986 corresponds to the new index 1980=100. The other periods correspond to the old index 1969=100.

cases we have a relative recovery reaching the already low output levels of 1981.

Finally in Table 5.6 column 2, we show that most of these sectors are working with low levels of idle capacity. As explained before, this is also a characteristic of the rest of the manufacturing groups.

Characteristics of Industrial Growth

In this section we analyze the effects of the recovery on the industrial structure. The objective is to identify those manufacturing groups with relatively higher rates of growth, thus contributing more to industrial recovery.

In Table 5.7 we classified into three categories those groups that, according to the new SOFOFA index, had an average annual growth rate greater than 10 percent during the recovery period of 1983–1986. In Category A we present those groups that mainly responded to those measures which changed relative prices in favor of the production of tradable goods. Particularly important were the maxi-devaluation of

TABLE 5.8 Growth of Manufacturing Output by Groups According to Destination: 1981-1986

Groups According to Destination	1981-86	1982-86
Regular Consumer Goods	1.0	4.2
Durable Consumer Goods	-8.9	7.4
Transport Equipment	-11.4	2.2
Capital Goods	0.04	11.5
Intermediate Goods for Industry	3.7	3.7
Intermediate Goods for Construction	-1.2	10.9
Intermediate Goods for Mining	3.5	10.4
Intermediate Goods for Silviculture	12.9	14.1
Packing and Accessories	3.6	8.6
Energy, Fuel and Lubricants	-1.0	4.1
Furniture	-2.5	2.5
Total Industry	1.2	5.4

Source: SOFOFA: Indice de Produccion Industrial (1980=100).

June 1982, the maintenance of a high real exchange rate, and the increase in tariffs. These measures favored those groups which were more affected by the rapid opening to trade implemented during 1976–1982.[7] In Category A we find the groups Textiles, Electrical Appliances and Housewares, Rubber Products, and Professional Equipment.

In Category B of Table 5.7 we find the majority of those groups that SOFOFA classified as producing intermediate goods for construction. As mentioned before, this was due to those policies which promoted the construction of housing and of new infrastructure within firms. The success of these manufacturing groups was strongly linked to the increase in government expenditures for public infrastructure. It is well known that because of its characteristics (relatively labor intensive and high backward linkages), construction is one of the preferred sectors to stimulate the economy after a severe crisis.

Finally, in Category C of Table 5.7, we present the groups Industrial Chemical and Miscellaneous Petroleum and Coal. In the former case, its growth was mainly associated with the production of fertilizers and insecticides, i.e. intermediate goods for agriculture, which, as mentioned before, was also a leading sector during the recovery. The growth of Miscellaneous Petroleum and Coal was probably associated with the general growth of industry, because it produces inputs, such as oil lubricants and grease, which are used in most manufacturing production processes.

In Table 5.8 we present the growth of industrial production by groups according to destiny of products, as given in the new SOFOFA index (1980=100). This information allows us to mention two more characteristics of the industrial recovery. In the first place is the important recovery of the capital goods producing sector. However, in this case it is important to consider that the 1981 levels were very much below the ones of the 1960s. In the second place is the high rate of growth of sectors producing intermediate goods for mining and silviculture. These are inputs that are used mainly by exporting sectors. Thus, part of the industrial recovery was linked to the recovery of sectors which had been traditional exports, such us mining, forestry, fruit, and agro-industry.

It is interesting to observe that the backward linkage effect is not concentrated in some sectors; rather, its impact reaches different sectors producing a great variety of goods. For instance, in the category Intermediate Goods for Silviculture, the production of the following goods is classified: fish meal which belongs to the food sector, insecticides and fertilizers belonging to the chemical products sector, and tools such as plows, shovels, etc., belonging to the metal production sector. This means that the importance of this effect within each sector is probably low as a share of total sector production. However, as shown in Table 5.8, the aggregation of these effects has been important during the industrial recovery since the 1982 crisis.

Conclusions

The main conclusion of this chapter is that the performance of the manufacturing sector during the 1983–1986 recovery reinforces our previous conclusion that a deindustrialization process took place during 1975–1982.

In spite of the fact that the industrial sector played an important role during the recovery, in terms of its contribution to output and employment growth, its capacity output has remained stagnant during the last 15 years. The evidence shows that the recovery was based on the utilization of the idle capacity created during the recession of 1982.

The analysis of those manufacturing sectors which were relatively more affected by deindustrialization shows that during the recovery, all these sectors had maximum capacity outputs below their already deteriorated capacities of the 1974–1981 period. Moreover, in most cases, the output of these sectors in 1986 was still below the levels of 1981.

The evidence, however, also shows that in spite of the fact that the textiles sector was one of the most deteriorated during the monetarist experience, it was able to recover at extraordinarily high rates. This suggests that those textile firms which were able to survive the 1982 crisis went through a process of reconversion of their productive capacities, which brought about their rapid recovery.

Finally, analyzing the characteristics of the leading sectors during the recovery, it is possible to conclude that industry responded to the following measures implemented after the 1982 crisis. First, the change in relative prices in favor of the tradable sector, which allowed for a recovery of industrial competitiveness. Second, an active fiscal policy, which was implemented particularly in the area of public infrastructure and housing. Third, financial measures which aimed to ease the burden on private domestic banks and firms; and fourth, the reduction of real wages which also contributed to the recovery of firms' profitability. Thus, the recovery of Chilean industry was based primarily on domestic measures, specifically a combination of import substitution and aggregate demand policies.

Notes

1. See the section on "The Chilean Economic Policy Context" in Chapter 1 for a detailed analysis of these issues.
2. The difference between both sources is the methodology in the estimation procedures. The Central Bank uses the "constant productivity method" and Marcel and Meller (1986) the "double deflation method."
3. See the section on "Opening Domestic Markets to International Trade" in Chapter 3 for a detailed analysis.
4. In Chapter 2 we present different hypotheses to explain the behavior of entrepreneurs regarding employees laid off in the two crises.
5. See the section on "The Evolution of Industrial Productive Capacity: 1969–1983" in Chapter 2 for a complete description of the methodology.
6. As mentioned in Chapter 2, considering the purpose of this study, there are at least four reasons which justify the exclusion of this sector. First is the heavy weight it has in the SOFOFA index (13.1 and 12.7 percent according to the old and new indexes respectively). Second is the fact that this sector is basically oriented to external markets. Third, the production of this sector has expanded every year since 1969 (with the exception of 1982); and fourth, one of the objectives of this study is to isolate the behavior of those sectors which were relatively more affected by the economic model imposed in 1973.
7. See the section on "Opening Domestic Markets to International Trade" in Chapter 3 for identification of the sources of structural change. See also Gatica and Pollack (1986).

Conclusions and Implications of the Study

The Chilean manufacturing sector was severely affected by the neo-conservative experiment implemented during the period 1974–1982. The sequence and intensity of the policies varied, but four factors seem to be the main determinants of the performance of the industrial sector during these years.

First were the changes on the level of industrial activity produced by restrictions on domestic demand. Particularly important was the tight monetary policy followed during the whole period and the rapid decline in government expenditures. The reduction in the role of the public sector was also a significant factor. Second, the rapid opening to international trade accompanied by a fixed exchange rate policy led to a loss of international competitiveness, amplifying the negative impact on import substitution activities and deteriorating the sector's export capacity. Third, the domestic liberalization of capital markets led to positive and extremely high real interest rates, which, among other things, produced unsustainable financial burdens, increasing the number of firms going bankrupt.

The last factor explaining the deterioration of the industrial sector was the change in the "system of incentives" in the economy. The loss of competitiveness shifted resources to non-tradable sectors and allowed incomes associated with imports to increase. The extraordinarily high interest rates moved resources away from productive activities towards short-run financial speculation, as the rates of return offered by the latter were impossible to attain in the former. In other words, the "system of incentives" was biased against productive investment and strongly encouraged financial investment of a speculative nature.

Overall, the performance of the Chilean manufacturing sector between 1974 and 1982 was the result of the application of a set of economic policies whose success depended on the achievement of a particular resource re-allocation pattern, that in reality did not occur. Because the economic authorities insisted on those policies, the costs associated with this pattern . . . in terms of unemployed resources and loss of potential output . . . were extraordinarily high. The variables did not respond as fast and sometimes not even in the direction expected.

The result was like a car suddenly going backwards when the intention of the driver was to go forward. Note, however, that the Chilean case is not the typical one, i.e. when the driver puts the car in reverse by mistake. The Chilean experience was more like a driver just learning to operate his/her brand new car who has to look at the owner's manual to see which gear should be used to go forward. The driver follows the instructions correctly, but when he/she presses the accelerator the car lurches backwards, smashes into the garage wall, and needs expensive repairs to put it back on the road again.

What happened? Why did the car go backwards in spite of the fact that the driver followed the instructions correctly? Very simply, the manual was wrong; the authors had made a big mistake. The assumptions used to write the manual did not make adjustments for the specific characteristics of the Chilean economy. So when the economic authorities of the time carefully followed the manual and pressed the accelerator, the economy went backwards, leaving behind massive unemployment and a country with one of the highest per capita external debts in the world.

Regarding the manufacturing sector, the neoconservative experiment produced a deindustrialization process which had the following characteristics:

A decline in the share of industrial output and employment in total GDP and total employment respectively. An absolute loss of manufacturing jobs and a decline in output to pre-1970 levels. Because these results were not the outcome of a generalized international pattern, nor a continuation of an historical tendency, it can be argued that this contraction was determined mainly by the particular policies followed during the monetarist experiment.

The costs of this experiment in terms of industrial output and employment were extremely high. If industry had maintained the annual average growth rate of the 1960s (5.7 percent), industrial output would have been 10 billion dollars greater in 1982 and industrial employment 35 percent greater than what was effectively realized in 1982.

Not only were manufacturing jobs destroyed, but productive capacity was also reduced. Between the two periods (1969–1973) and (1982–1983), maximum production capacity decreased by 9.5 percent and, excluding the refining of copper and other non-ferrous metals, productive capacity was reduced by 19.2 percent.

These results are substantiated by the fact that, compared with the second half of the 1960s, the average number of total bankruptcies more than doubled during the monetarist experiment and the share of manufacturing bankruptcies in total bankruptcies increased from an average of 8.4 percent to 24.6 percent. Additionally, the number of bankruptcies seems to be a consistent indicator of the degree and intensity of the deindustrialization process. In approximately 95 percent of the cases the productive plants of bankrupt firms were dismantled, reducing the productive capacity of these firms.

Another indicator of the degree of deindustrialization shows that the number of establishments decreased by 29.4 percent between 1967 and 1982. This decline was concentrated in the last years of this period. During 1967–1979, the number of establishments fell by only 8.5 percent, while during 1979–1982 this same percentage was 22.9 percent.

A closer look at the evolution of manufacturing employment shows that between 1967 and 1982 the drop in manufacturing employment reached the stunning figure of 31.8 percent, which means that employment declined at an average annual rate of 2.5 percent. Breaking down that period of time into 1967–1979 and 1979–1982, the results show that in the former employment decreased by 5.2 percent, while in the latter it dropped precipitously by 28.0 percent.

A complete series of statistics on manufacturing employment for the period 1967–1982 exists only for firms employing more than 50 workers. The results show that between 1967 and 1973, industrial employment was increasing at an average annual rate of 2.1 percent. Manufacturing employment fell at an average annual rate of 6.2 percent every year of the monetarist experiment (1974–1982), with 1977 the only exception.

An analysis disaggregated at the three-digit level (ISIC rev. 2) for all the indicators mentioned in the previous points (employment, number of bankruptcies and establishments, and productive capacity), shows that those manufacturing groups most affected by the deindustrialization phenomenon were the ones producing: (a) regular finished consumer goods like textiles, wearing apparel, leather and footwear, (b) durable consumer goods and intermediate goods for construction, like metal products, machinery and electrical machinery, (c) transport equipment and (d) miscellaneous manufacturing goods like professional and scientific equipment.

Moreover, the performance of these groups after the 1982 crisis (i.e. the period 1983–1986) shows that they had maximum capacity outputs below their already deteriorated capacities of the 1974–1981 period.

Furthermore, in most cases, the output of these sectors in 1986 was still below the levels of 1981.

Deindustrialization was not the outcome of a movement of resources towards greater economic efficiency. The loss of employment in manufacturing did not lead to redeployment to other activities, but only to increases in overall unemployment. The ability of the sector to generate foreign exchange worsened, thus increasing the severe disequilibrium in the country's external commercial balance. The rate of investment decreased relative to its historical levels, and labor productivity does not seem to have increased above those figures observed in the past.

The opening to international trade was one of the most important structural policies implemented during the neoconservative experiment. Tariffs were rapidly reduced and non-tariff barriers were completely eliminated. At the same time, the manufacturing sector was affected by domestic demand restrictions. A methodology which allows separating the sources of structural change among changes in domestic demand, in exports, and in import substitution was applied to manufacturing groups disaggregated at a three-digit level.

The results for the period 1967–1982 showed that the dominant influence among those sectors that increased output was domestic demand, with the exception of the food and paper sector where the expansion of exports was the main source of output growth. In the case of wood, exports played a major role in avoiding further drops in output.

Those groups where output decreased can be separated into three categories. First, those groups which were negatively affected by domestic demand restrictions and the opening to international trade. Most of these groups produce regular consumer goods. Second, those groups producing intermediate goods for construction, transport equipment and miscellaneous manufacturing goods, which were primarily affected by restrictions in aggregate demand. Third were two groups producing non-electrical machinery and professional and scientific equipment, which suffered severely under a process of desubstitution of imports.

Among those manufacturing groups most affected by deindustrialization, the majority belonged to the first category, i.e. groups producing regular consumer goods affected by both demand restriction and desubstitution of imports. However, demand restriction was the main source of deterioration in the case of metal products and transportation equipment. Finally, two groups (machinery and scientific equipment) were mainly affected by the opening-up process, as evidenced by the fact that they experienced a positive contribution of domestic demand, accompanied by a significant increase in imports and a fall in output.

Another source of industrial deterioration was the domestic liberalization of capital markets and the opening-up to international financial markets. These reforms had important effects on the functioning of manufacturing firms. A comparison between the financial behavior of bankrupt firms with firms that survived shows that one of the mechanisms used by the latter was to maintain a high proportion of total assets in a financial form. This was done so as to take advantage of extraordinarily high interest rates, and to effectively postpone productive investment decisions.

These results were supported by the findings of a case study, where the financial management of firms that survived was compared with that of firms that went bankrupt. The financial reforms were an important determinant of the number of bankrupt firms. A comparison of liquidity, profitability and indebtedness ratios of bankrupt firms with those of surviving firms shows that the former experienced a combination of relatively high debt, low liquidity and negative profitability ratios, accompanied by greater shares of financial expenditures in total sales and negative operational and non-operational net income ratios, which made their productive activities unfeasible.

The performance of the industrial sector after the 1982 crisis, i.e. during the 1983–1986 recovery, reinforces the idea that the Chilean deindustrialization process was not just the result of cyclical reductions in industrial production. The magnitude and intensity of this process was much broader and deeper. The destruction of manufacturing jobs and the deterioration of productive capacity reduced the relative importance of industry in the economy, thus reducing the capacity of the sector to respond in the eventual economic recovery. This fact constitutes the starting point of any industrial redevelopment strategy.

The available evidence regarding the role industry played during the recovery shows that deindustrialization introduces an additional constraint to short-term economic improvement, in the sense that a process of industrial recovery cannot be entirely based on the use of idle capacity. In spite of the existence of idle capacity, part of the decline in employment and industrial production is the consequence of plant closings and eroded capital equipment, due to the drop in investment rates.

If the recovery depended only upon using that capacity which was previously idle, then the rate of growth would depend simply on demand restrictions and input availability. However, deindustrialization inhibits the growth process because productive capacity has been reduced. In short, deindustrialization introduces an additional supply bottleneck which inhibits expanding output, consequently reducing the sector's ability to create employment.

In a study made for PREALC (1984) we pursued this argument a little further. The objective was to analyze to what extent the existence of idle capacity in the manufacturing sector could reduce the possibilities of a future recovery. The results showed that in 1983 total industry was using around 80 percent of its installed capacity. However, a more disaggregated analysis (three-digit ISIC rev. 2) showed that those manufacturing groups that were most affected by the deindustrialization process had the least amount of excess capacity in 1983. This was due to the fact that these groups suffered the greatest deterioration in productive capacity. This was especially the case of groups producing regular finished consumer goods.

The existence of short-run supply bottlenecks for expanding output brings us next to those issues that are related to the possibility of increasing investment. If the current situation is characterized by a combination of reduced productive capacity and low levels of idle capacity, then in order to raise output, the rate of investment must increase. However, as noted before, the availability of foreign exchange is one of the major constraints facing the Chilean economy today. On the other hand, the possibilities for increasing domestic savings are slim. Most firms are still substantially in debt and per capita income is still below the levels of 1965. Undoubtedly, the severe deterioration experienced by the manufacturing sector puts additional pressure on the balance of payments, especially since foreign resources are scarce and investment is badly needed to increase the level of industrial activity.

The Chilean economy is still recovering from the crisis in 1982, one of its most severe of the present century. By the early 1990s, it should be clear whether this crisis can be overcome with a new strategic perspective, or if we will continue with the type of short-run adjustments and cyclical accommodations without long-run vision. For the manufacturing sector, the problem is not only to increase the level of industrial activity, but also to strengthen its technological and productive base, in order to establish new ways of relating to the world economy and of reducing the present levels of vulnerability.

Together with implementing measures to reduce foreign financial constraints, deliberate policies to strengthen the actual productive capacity of the country should be undertaken. Short-run adjustment policies should be viewed as part of a broader and wider process of industrial restructuring. In other words, the present crisis will not be overcome by implementing adjustment policies aimed at returning to the best time of the neoconservative period, nor to the pre-1973 years. The results of this research suggest that the crisis has been too severe to allow expectations that policies designed to deal with cyclical economic problems will give positive results in the medium and long-run. To overcome the present crisis, the whole concept of industrial development needs to be modified.

These modifications include the understanding that the type of adjustments proposed by foreign banks and international agencies shoud be critically assessed. Usually these propositions underestimate the importance of external factors, forcing the domestic economy to shoulder most of the burden of the adjustment process. The results are often severe domestic recessions and a very slow process of economic recovery. The reason is that implicit in these views is what has been called the "locomotive effect," i.e. that a major factor determining the recovery of the economy is the growth process in the developed countries. Also implicit in these views is the idea that the manufacturing sector is not more important than other sectors, like agriculture or services. They believe the rules of the game should be the same for all. This is why explicit references to the development of the industrial sector are almost always absent in these propositions.

Given Chile's large external debt, the scarcity of foreign exchange is a very important factor determining the future development of the economy. Manufacturing's ability to generate and save foreign exchange should thus make it one of the priorities of an industrialization strategy. The challenge is to establish new ways of relating to the world economy, while at the same time softening the impact of external factors on the domestic economy. The issue is not to reduce the importance of the external sector in the economy, but to diminish the negative impact of external shocks through a diversification of export goods and trading partners. This new role should be based on a more integrated industrial and technological structure and on a more autonomous capacity to innovate.

An interesting characteristic of the international crisis of the early 1980s is that those Latin American countries that showed the greatest capacity to react to the crisis were also the ones that had greater, more extended and integrated productive bases. Thus, with their productive capacity they were able to react promptly to the need to substitute for imports and increase exports. An important conclusion from these experiences is the strategic need to expand investment and to strengthen the technological capacity of the economy. Another key point is the need to accelerate the growth of industrial exports through the development of the interregional market. This space can be used first as a platform for the development of industrial exports, henceforth jumping to more sophisticated and larger markets after successful product development and promotion in the regional sphere.

As the results of Chapter 3 demonstrated, the importance of expanding the domestic market should also be stressed. This should also be a crucial element of the strategy, not only to develop selective import substitution but also to improve the well-being of the majority of the population. Massive unemployment and increasing poverty are urgent problems of the Chilean economy. A reindustrialization process can help to overcome these problems by creating jobs and increasing the production of basic goods.

As discussed above, the issues regarding the implications of the deindustrialization process are very much related to those issues concerning a reindustrialization strategy for the Chilean economy. In spite of the fact that this latter issue is among the most important ones for the future development of Chile, it obviously goes well beyond the objective of this book. However, it is my hope that this study of deindustrialization contributes new insights to the reindustrialization debate.

Bibliography

Aedo, C., and Lagos, L.F. "Protección Efectiva en Chile, 1974–1979," *Documento de Trabajo,* No. 94, Departamento de Economía Universidad Católica de Chile, Agosto, 1984.

Agrupación de Economistas Socialistas. "Una Estrategia de Reindustrialización: Notas Preliminares." *Colección Chileconómico,* No. 4, Centro de Estudios Económicos y Sociales, VECTOR, Septiembre, 1986.

Aninat, A. "Sector Textil: Transformaciones y Potencialidades." In *La Industria Chilena: Cuatro Visiones Sectoriales,* Centro de Estudios del Desarrollo, CED, 1986.

Arellano, J.P., and Cortazar, R. "Del Milagro a la Crisis: Algunas Reflexiones Sobre el Momento Económico," *Colección Estudios CIEPLAN,* No. 8, Julio, 1982.

Banco Interamericano de Desarrollo (ed.). *Industrialización y Desarrollo en América Latina.* Banco Interamericano de Desarrollo, Washington, D.C., 1983.

Bitar, S. "Crisis Financiera e Industrialización de América Latina." Unpublished Manuscript. Secretaría Permanente del Sistema Económico Latinoamericano, Enero, 1985.

Blackaby, F. (ed.). *De-Industrialization.* London: Heinemann Educational Books, 1979.

Bluestone, B., and Harrison, B., *The Deindustrialization of America.* New York: Basic Books, 1982.

Bluestone, B., Harrison, B., and Baker, L. *Corporate Flight: The Causes and Consequences of Economic Dislocation.* Washington, D.C.: Progressive Alliance Book, 1981.

Boyer, R., and Petit, P. "Employment and Productivity in the EEC," *Cambridge Journal of Economics,* March, 1981.

Brown, C.F.J., and Sheriff, T.D. "De-Industrialisation: A Background Paper." In *De-Industrialisation.* Edited by Frank Blackaby. London: Heinemann Educational Books, 1979.

Cairncross, A. "What is De-Industrialization?" In *De-Industrialization.* Edited by Frank Blackaby. London: Heinemann Educational Books, 1979.

Carter, A.P. *Structural Change in the American Economy.* Cambridge, Massachusetts: Harvard University Press, 1970.

Castillo, M., "Generación de Empleo y Sectores Industriales Claves," *Materiales Para Discusión,* No. 5, Centro de Estudios del Desarrollo, CED, Mayo, 1984.

Castillo, M., and Tardito, C. "Simulación de Impactos de Reactivación en Chile," *Material Para Discusión,* No. 6, Centro de Estudios del Desarrollo, CED, Junio, 1984.

Castillo, M. "Situación y Perspectivas de la Industria Alimentaria." In *La Industria Chilena: Cuatro Visiones Sectoriales.* Centro de Estudios del Desarrollo, CED, 1986.

CEPAL. "Dos Estudios Sobre Endeudamiento Externo," *Cuadernos de la CEPAL,* No. 19, Naciones Unidas, 1978.

_____. "Estabilización y Liberalización Económica en el Cono Sur," *Estudios e Informe,* No. 38, Agosto, 1984.

Chenery, H. *Structural Change and Development Policy.* Oxford University Press, 1980.

CIEPLAN. *Reconstrucción Económica Para la Democracia.* 3ra. ed., Santiago: Editorial Aconcagua, 1984.

Cline, W., and Weintraub, S. (eds.). *Economic Stabilization in Developing Countries.* Washington, D.C.: Brookings Intitution, 1981.

Corbo, V. "Recent Developments of the Chilean Economy." Unpublished Manuscript. Instituto de Economía, Universidad Católica de Chile, 1982.

_____. "The Current Account and the Trade Balance: The Case of Chile." Unpublished Manuscript. Instituto de Economía, Universidad Católica de Chile, Febrero, 1982.

Corbo, V., and Meller, P. "Alternative Trade Strategies and Employment Implications: Chile." In *Trade and Employment in Developing Countries: Individual Studies.* Edited by A. Krueger. Chicago: University of Chicago Press, 1981.

Corbo, V., and Sanchez, J. M. "Impact on Firms of the Liberalization and Stabilization Policies in Chile: Some Case Studies." Unpublished Manuscript. Instituto de Economía, Universidad Católica de Chile, Abril, 1984.

Corbo, V., and Pollack, M. "Una Estimación de las Tarifas Nominales del Sector Industrial en el Año 1967," Unpublished Manuscript. Departamento de Estudio Empresas B.H.C., 1979.

_____. "Fuentes del Cambio en la Estructura Económica Chilena: 1960–1979," *Estudios de Economía,* Departamento de Economía, Universidad de Chile, Primer Semestre 1982.

Cortazar, R. "Distribución del Ingreso, Empleo y Remuneraciones Reales en Chile, 1970–1978." *Colección Estudios CIEPLAN* No. 3, Junio, 1980.

_____. "Desempleo, Pobreza y Distribución: Chile 1970–1981," *Apuntes CIEPLAN* 34, Junio, 1982.

_____. "Chile: Distributive Results 1973–1982." Unpublished Manuscript. CIEPLAN, 1982.

_____."El Mercado del Trabajo y las Políticas de Estabilización." Unpublished Manuscript. CIEPLAN, 1983.

Cortazar, R., Foxley, A., and Tokman, V. *Legados del Monetarismo, Argentina y Chile,* Buenos Aires: Ediciones Solar, 1984.

Cortazar, R., and Marshall, J. "Indice de Precios al Consumidor en Chile: 1970–1978," *Colección Estudios CIEPLAN* No. 4, Noviembre, 1980.

Cripps, T.F., and Tarling, R.J. *Growth in Advanced Capitalist Economies 1950–1970.* Cambridge: Cambridge University Press, 1973.

Dahse, F. *Mapa de la Extrema Riqueza. Los Grupos Económicos y el Proceso de Concentración de Capitales.* Santiago: Editorial Aconcagua, 1979.

Diario Oficial de la República de Chile, Ley de Quiebras Número 18.175, Santiago, 28 de Octubre, 1982.

Diaz-Alejandro, C. "Southern Cone Stabilization Plans." In *Economic Stabilization in Developing Countries.* Edited by Cline, W., and Weintraub, S. Washington, D.C.: Brookings Institution, 1981.

Dornbusch, R. *Open Economy Macroeconomics.* New York: Basic Books, 1980.

Dornbusch, R., and Fischer, S. *Macroeconomics.* 2nd ed. New York: McGraw-Hill, 1981.

Dornbusch, R. "Stabilization Policy in Developing Countries: What Have We Learned?" *World Development,* Special Issue, 1982.

Duran, H. "La Industria en Chile, 1970–1979," *Documento de Trabajo,* CEPAL/ONVDI, División de Desarrollo Industrial, Noviembre, 1980.

Edwards, S. "Economic Policy and the Record of Economic Growth in Chile in the 1970's and 1980's." Unpublished Manuscript. UCLA, Department of Economics, 1982.

_____. "Trade Liberalization, Minimum Wages and Employment in the Short Run: Some Reflections Based on the Chilean Experience." *Working Paper* No. 230, UCLA, Department of Economics, February, 1982.

Errazuriz, E. "Industrial Development in Chile. The Restructuring of Industry 1973–1981 and Elements for an Alternative Strategy Within a Democratic Perspective." Institute of Social Studies, La Haya, 1982.

Espinosa, N. Gonzalez, I. "La Quiebra de Empresas en Chile. Periodo 1975–1982." Unpublished Magister Dissertation. Escuela de Administración, Universidad de Chile, 1982.

Fajnzylber, F. *La Industrialización Trunca de América Latina.* Mexico: Editorial Nueva Imagen, 1983.

Ffrench-Davis, R. "Exportaciones e Industrialización en un Modelo Ortodojo: Chile 1973–1978," *Revista de la CEPAL* No. 9, Diciembre, 1979.

_____. "Liberalización de Importaciones: La Experiencia Chilena en 1973–1979," *Colección Estudios CIEPLAN* No. 4, Noviembre, 1980.

Ffrench-Davis, R., and Arellano, J.P. "Apertura Financiera Externa: La Experiencia Chilena en 1973–1980," *Colección Estudios CIEPLAN* No. 5, Julio, 1981.

Ffrench-Davis, R. (ed). "Deuda Externa, Industrialización y Ahorro en América Latina." *Colección Estudios CIEPLAN* No. 17, Septiembre, 1985.

Flaño N. "La Recesión y el Ajuste Automático: Una Visión Crítica," *Apuntes CIEPLAN* No. 32, Mayo, 1982.

Foxley, A. "Hacia Una Economía de Libre Mercado: Chile 1970–1978," *Colección Estudios CIEPLAN* No. 4, Noviembre, 1980.

_____. *Latin American Experiments in Neoconservative Economics.* Berkeley, California: University of California Press, 1983.

_____. "Enfoques Ortodojos para el Ajuste Económico de Corto Plazo: Lecciones de la Experiencia y Temas de Investigación." In *Industrialización y*

Desarrollo en América Latina. Editado por el Banco Interamericano de Desarrollo, Washington, D.C., 1983.

Garcia, A. "Industrialización para el Desarrollo Equitativo," *Monografia sobre Empleo* No. 39, PREALC/ISS, Octubre, 1984.

Garcia, A., and Gatica, J. "Reindustrialización: Una Condición para el Desarrollo," *Colección Chileconómico* No. 4, Centro de Estudios Económicos y Sociales, VECTOR, Septiembre, 1986.

Garcia, N. "Industria Manufacturera y Empleo: América Latina 1950–1980," *PREALC Trabajos Ocasionales* No. 49, Septiembre, 1982.

Garcia N., and Marfan M. "Incidencia Indirecta de la Industrialización Latinoamericana Sobre el Empleo," *PREALC Trabajos Ocasionales* No. 38, Noviembre, 1982.

Gatica, J. "The Performance of the Manufacturing Sector in Chile, 1974–1982: A Case of De-Industrialization." Ph.D. Dissertation, University of Notre Dame, USA.

Gatica, J., Romaguera, P., and Romero, L.R. "Un Indice de la Escala Unica de Remuneraciones del Sector Público Chileno 1974–1986," *Revista de Análisis Económico,* Vol. 2, No. 2, Programa de Postgrado en Economía. Ilades/Georgetown University, Noviembre, 1987.

Gatica, J., and Pollack, M. "Las Fuentes del Cambio en la Estructura del Sector Industrial Chileno: 1967–1982," *Estudios de Economía,* Vol. 13, No. 2, Facultad de Ciencias Económicas y Administrativas, Departamento de Economía, Universidad de Chile, Diciembre, 1986.

Gatica, J., and Uthoff, A. "Determinantes Estructurales y Coyunturales de la Producción en la Industria Manufacturera Chilena: 1969–1983," In *Perspectivas Económicas para la Democracia: Balance y Lecciones para la Experiencia Chilena,* edited by J. Rodriguez, Instituto Chileno de Estudios Humanísticos, ICHEH, Santiago, 1984.

Goodman, R. *The Last Entrepreneurs: America's Regional Wars for Jobs and Dollars.* New York: Simon and Schuster, 1979.

Herrera, J.E., and Morales, J. "La Inversión Financiera Externa: El Caso de Chile, 1974–1978," *Colección Estudios CIEPLAN* No. 1, Julio, 1979.

Jadresic, E. "Evolución del Empleo y Desempleo en Chile, 1970–1985." *Colección Estudios CIEPLAN* No. 20, Diciembre, 1986.

Jimenez, F. "Peru: La Expansión del Sector Manufacturero como Generadora de Crecimiento Económico y el Papel del Sector Externo," *Socialismo y Participación* No. 18, 1982.

Kaldor, N. *Causes of the Slow Rate of Economic Growth of the United Kingdom.* Cambridge: Cambridge University Press, 1966.

______. *Strategic Factors in Economic Development.* Ithaca, Cornell University, 1967.

______. "Comment on Cairncross, A. What is De-Industrialization." In Blackaby, F. *De-Industrialization.* London: Heinemann Educational Books, 1979.

Klein, L.R., and Summers, R. *The Wharton Index of Capacity Utilization,* University of Pennsylvania, 1966.

Lagos, R., and Tokman, V. "Monetarismo Global, Empleo y Estratificación Social," *Trabajo Ocasional* No. 47, PREALC, Julio, 1982.

Marcel, M., and Meller, P. "Empalme de las Cuentas Nacionales de Chile 1960–1985. Metodos Alternativos y Resultados." *Colección Estudios CIEPLAN* No. 20, Diciembre, 1986.

Marshall, J. "El Gasto Público en Chile: 1969–1979," *Colección Estudios CIEPLAN* No. 5, Julio, 1981.

Marshall, J., and Romaguera, P. "La Evolución del Empleo Público en Chile, 1970–1978," *Notas Técnicas CIEPLAN* No. 26, Febrero, 1981.

Martner, G. (ed). *El Pensamiento Económico del Gobierno de Allende.* Editorial Universitaria, Santiago, 1971.

McKinnon, R. "The Order of Economic Liberalization: Lessons from Chile and Argentina," *Research Center in Economic Growth Memorandum* No. 251, Stanford University, January, 1982.

_____. "La Intermediación Financiera y el Control Monetario en Chile," *Cuadernos de Economía* No. 43, Departamento de Economía, Universidad Católica de Chile Diciembre, 1977.

Meller, P., Cortazar, R., and Marshall, J. "La Evolución del Empleo en Chile: 1974–1978," *Colección Estudios CIEPLAN* No. 2, Diciembre, 1979.

Meller, P., Livacich, E., and Arrau, P. "Una Revisión del Milagro Económico Chileno (1976–1981)," *Colección Estudios CIEPLAN* No. 15, Diciembre, 1984.

Mizala, A. "Liberalización Financiera y Quiebra de Empresas Industriales: Chile, 1977–1982," *Notas Técnicas CIEPLAN* No. 67, Enero, 1985.

Muñoz, O., Gatica, J., and Romaguera P. "Crecimiento y Estructura del Empleo Estatal en Chile, 1940–1970," *Notas Técnicas CIEPLAN* No. 22, Santiago, Enero, 1980.

Muñoz, O. "Hacia Una Nueva Industrialización. Elementos de Estrategia de Desarrollo para una Democracia," *El Trimestre Económico,* No. 200, 1983.

_____. "Crecimiento y Desequilibrio en una Economia Abierta: El Caso Chileno 1976–1981," *Colección Estudios CIEPLAN* No. 8, Julio, 1982.

Ominami, C. "Desindustrialización y Reestructuración Industrial en América Latina." *Colección Estudios CIEPLAN* No. 23, Marzo, 1988.

Phan-Thuy, N., Betancourt, R.R., Winston, G.C., and Kabaj, M. *Industrial Capacity and Employment Promotion.* England: Gower, 1981.

Phillips, A. "An Appraisal of Measures of Capacity," *American Economic Review,* Supplement 53, 1963.

Pinto, A. "Chile: El Modelo Ortodoxo y el Desarrollo Nacional," *El Trimestre Económico,* No. 192, Octubre-Diciembre, 1981.

_____. "Centro-Periferia e Industrialización. Vigencias y Cambios en el Pensamiento de la CEPAL," *El Trimestre Económico,* Número Especial, Abril-Junio, 1983.

PREALC. "Políticas de Estabilización y Empleo en América Latina," *Investigaciones Sobre Empleo* No. 22, 1982.

_____. "Monetarismo Global y Respuesta Industrial: El Caso de Argentina," *Documento de Trabajo* No. 231, Diciembre, 1983.

_____. "Monetarismo Global y Respuesta Industrial: El Caso de Chile," *Documento de Trabajo* No. 232, Marzo, 1984.

_____. "Monetarismo Global y Respuesta Industrial: El Caso de Uruguay," *Documento de Trabajo* No. 233, Marzo, 1984.

______. "Una Nota Sobre el Impacto de la Liberalización y Apertura Financiera Sobre el Sector Manufacturero Chileno: 1974–1982." *Documento de Trabajo* No. 275, Abril, 1986.

______. "Nuevos Antecedentes Sobre la Desindustrialización Chilena," *Documento de Trabajo* No. 307, Octubre, 1987.

Rakowski, J. "Unproductive Investment and the Diversion of Capital from Productive Investment." Unpublished Manuscript. Department of Economics, University of Notre Dame.

Ramos, J. "The Economics of Hyperstagflation: Stabilization Policy in Post 1973 Chile," *Journal of Development Economics*, July, 1980.

Riveros, L. "Un Análisis Sobre el Problema del Empleo en Chile en la Década del 70," *Estudios de Economía* No. 23. Departamento de Economía, Universidad de Chile, Octubre, 1984.

Sanfuentes, A. "Políticas de Empleo de Largo Plazo para Chile," *Documento de Investigación* No. 62, Departamento de Economía, Universidad de Chile, 1983.

Scherman, J. "La Industria Textil y de Prendas de Vestir y la Apertura al Exterior: Chile 1974–1978." Unpublished Manuscript. CIEPLAN, Octubre, 1980.

Schydlowsky, D. "International Trade Policy in the Economic Growth of Latin America," *Discussion Paper Series* No. 5, CLADS, Boston University, May, 1973.

Singh, A. "U.K. Industry and the World Economy: A Case of De-Industrialization," *Cambridge Journal of Economics*, Vol. 1, 1977.

______. *Third World Industrialization and the Structure of the World Economy.* Cambridge: Cambridge University Press, 1982.

Sjaastad, L., and Cortes, M. "El Enfoque Monetario de la Balanza de Pagos y las Tasas Reales de Interés en Chile," *Estudio de Economía* No. 11, Departamento de Economía, Universidad de Chile, 1978.

Tapia, D. "Apertura al Mercado Financiero Internacional," *Institucionalidad Económica e Integración Financiera con el Exterior*, Instituto de Estudios Bancarios, Santiago, 1979.

Tardito, C. "Revisión Crítica de las Estadísticas Industriales," *Material Para Discusión* No. 7, Centro de Estudios del Desarrollo, CED, Junio, 1984.

Thatcher, A.R. "Labor Supply and Employments Trends." In *De-Industrialization.* Edited by Blackaby, F. London: Heinemann Educational Books, 1979.

Tokman, V. "Monetarismo Global y Destrucción Industrial," *Revista CEPAL* No. 23, Agosto, 1984.

______. "Reactivación con Transformación: El Efecto Empleo." *Colección Estudios CIEPLAN* No. 14, Septiembre, 1984.

United Nations. *International Standard Industrial Classification of all Economic Activities.* Series M No. 4, rev. 2, New York: United Nations Publication, 1968.

Vazquez, A. "Crecimiento Económico y Productividad en la Industria Manufacturera," *Economía Mexicana* No. 3, CIDE, Mexico, 1981.

Vergara, P. "Apertura Externa y Desarrollo Industrial en Chile: 1973–1978," *Colección Estudios CIEPLAN* No. 4, Noviembre, 1980.

———. "Las Transformaciones de las Funciones Económicas del Estado en Chile Bajo el Régimen Militar," *Colección Estudios CIEPLAN,* No. 5, Julio, 1981.

Vignolo, C. "El Crecimiento Exportador y sus Perspectivas Bajo el Modelo Neoliberal Chileno." *Documento de Trabajo* No. 2, Centro de Estudios del Desarrollo, CED, 1983.

Wall Street Journal, May 5, 1983.

Weinstein, J. "La Industria en una Estrategia de Desarrollo para Chile," *Materiales Para Discusión* No. 33, Centro de Estudios del Desarrollo, CED, 1984.

Whitman, M.V.N. "Global Monetarism and the Monetary Approach to the Balance of Payments," *Brookings Papers on Economic Activity,* No. 3, 1975.

Zahler, R. "Repercusiones Monetarias y Reales de la Apertura Financiera al Exterior: El Caso Chileno 1975–1978," *Revista de la CEPAL* No. 10, Abril, 1980.

Index

For Product Safety Concerns and Information please contact our EU representative GPSR@taylorandfrancis.com Taylor & Francis Verlag GmbH, Kaufingerstraße 24, 80331 München, Germany

Batch number: 10726013

Printed by Printforce, the Netherlands